Unusual
Prophecies
Being Fulfilled

Unusual Prophecies Being Fulfilled

NEW INSIGHT INTO 9-11

REVEALING *the* PLANS *and* PROPHECIES *of* APOCALYPTIC MUSLIMS *and* FUTURE TERROR ATTACKS *in* AMERICA

Perry Stone

ISBN: 0-9708611-6-8
LOC: 2005908099

Voice of Evangelism Outreach Ministries
P.O. Box 3595
Cleveland, Tennessee, 37320
(423) 478-3456
Fax: 423-478-1392
www.Perrystone.org

Printed in the United States of America
Pathway Press, 1080 Montgomery Avenue,
Cleveland, Tennessee 37311

Contents

In evaluating 9/11, consider these

Islamic Prophecies of the End-time

If there are twenty* among you with determination, they will vanquish two hundred; if there are a hundred, they will slaughter a thousand unbelievers, for the infidels are people devoid of understanding (Qur'an 8:53).

Narrated Anas: When 'Abdullah bin Salam heard the arrival of the Prophet at Medina, he came to him and said, "What is the first portent of the Hour?" Allah's Apostle said, "The first portent of the Hour will be a fire that will bring together the people from the east to the west" (Hadith 4.55.546).

* *Twenty terrorists* were scheduled for the 9/11 attack, but one could not make it.

Introduction

It now seems like a bad dream, yet the entire world changed within 24 hours. On the morning of September 11, 2001, the workers at the World Trade Center arrived, preparing for another busy workday. The smell of fresh brewing coffee filtered through the offices, and the clicking sounds of computer mainframes prepared for the days activity at New York's famous Twin Towers.

Before the sun would set that day, the towers would be nonexistent, the streets near the towers covered in grey dust and the air filled with the smell of jet fuel and burning metal. Americans would be glued to their televisions in a state of shock, as citizens sought answers that could not be found.

By sunset a new war had begun—the unplanned and unexpected war on terrorism. The events of 9/11 had thrust America into an unwanted war on three fronts. The first front is a battle within the nation itself, to secure the homeland. It included exposing and arresting sleeper cells and developing new laws to help restrain terrorists from future attacks.

The second front would take American and coalition troops to the Taliban strongholds in the rugged terrain of Afghanistan. American forces would attempt to root out one of the fiercest Islamic terror organizations in the world, al Qaeda, and destroy the secret training camps headed by terror mastermind, Osama bin Laden.

The third front of this new war, designed to prevent future chemical and biological attacks, would take our military to the ancient territory of Babylon, today called Iraq, where Saddam Hussein, his sons and cronies, were planning to restart their chemical, biological and nuclear programs, posing a major threat to America, Europe, Israel and their allies.

There are two opinions on the issue of Islamic terrorism. Some optimists believe these fanatics of terror will eventually be defeated. Others acknowledge that the present situation creates a fresh breeding ground for new and younger terrorists, motivated by a desire to destroy what they call The Great Satan, or America, along with our friends, Great Britain and Israel.

After years of observation and research, I believe the Bible may reveal several ancient prophecies that are relevant in understanding terrorism. I believe they may explain how terrorists could fulfill these unusual prophecies penned thousands of years ago in Holy Scripture. When we compare these unique Bible prophecies with the possibilities for future terrorist activity, especially Islamic terrorist activity, we can now see how these passages of scripture could be fulfilled.

In this special book, Number Two in the series, *Unusual Prophecies Being Fulfilled*, I attempt to give the reader important insight into this subject, along with the scriptures and prophecies related to the times and seasons in which we live. I show how these prophetic utterances relate especially to Islamic terrorism.

I dedicate this book to those who are fighting the war on terror throughout the world. Your tireless efforts are not in vain.

A Servant of Christ

Perry Stone, Jr.

*I also will do this to you: I will even appoint terror over you. . . .
I will set My face against you, and you shall be defeated by your
enemies* (Leviticus 26:16, 17).

1

The Day the Countdown Began

On September 9, 2001, two days prior to September 11, missionary Luke Walters was traveling home from a village crusade on the island of Sri Lanka when he received a telephone call from his head intercessor, a Sri Lankan of Berger descent named Maureen Francke. When he answered his cell phone, Maureen began explaining to him that she had received a vision from the Lord which was disturbing her greatly. She was on a 40-day fast and had been in intense prayer.

Maureen said, "Pastor Luke, I saw two tall buildings in a large city; and two hands pushed the buildings to the ground, and a great cloud of white dust-like fire covered the whole city. People seemed to be walking on top of the clouds." She said she felt it was a city in America, but was uncertain of the full meaning of the vision.

She asked Luke what he thought it meant. He replied, "I have no idea." He suggested that she pray and ask God for the spiritual understanding. She also said that after the buildings fell, she saw a vision of the planet spinning; and suddenly, after the fall of the building, the planet (Earth) began to click like the sound of a clock. It appeared the fall of the buildings triggered the earth in the mode of a new prophetic countdown.

Maureen sketched the vision on a piece of paper and gave it to Luke. On September 11, Luke arrived home. His wife called on a cell phone and said someone had just flown an airplane into the World Trade Center.

Luke was sitting in front of the television when the second plane struck the second tower. Immediately Luke recalled Maureen's strange vision. Luke said, "Most of the Christian remnant in Sri Lanka have a burden to pray for their own country. However, Maureen was burdened for America!"

They Chose September 11

After the assault on America, many people questioned why the date, September 11, was chosen. Was it merely a coincidence or was there some cryptic meaning to the time? As individuals began researching the "why," some discovered interesting parallels in the number of times the number *11* was linked to the attacks.

♦ The date of the attack was 9-11; and 9 plus 1 plus 1 = 11

♦ September 11 is the 254th day of the year; and 2 plus 5 plus 4 = 11

♦ 119 is the area code of Oran/Iran; and 1 plus 1 plus 9 = 11

- The first plane that hit the North Tower was Flight 11.
- New York was the 11th state added to the Union.
- *New York City* has 11 letters.
- *Afghanistan* has 11 letters.
- *The Pentagon* has 11 letters.
- *Ramzi Yousef*, the terrorist who attacked the W.T.C. in 1993, has 11 letters in his name.
- Flight 11 had 92 people on board; 9 plus 2 = 11
- Flight 77 had 65 people on board; 6 plus 5 = 11
- The Twin Towers resembled the number 11 from a distance.

Another odd coincidence involved the number 20. Nineteen hijackers were directly connected to the two planes that flew into the Trade Center, the plane that hit the Pentagon and the plane that was headed to Washington D.C. before it crashed in Pennsylvania. There was, allegedly, a 20th hijacker named Zacarias Moussaoui, who was arrested on illegal immigration charges nearly a month before 9/11, and was unable to board one of the ill-fated planes.

An odd coincidence is linked to the $20-bill. While a guest on the Trinity Broadcasting Network (TBN) in January, 2002, I shared with viewers the strange image that appears on the back of a $20-bill when the currency is folded in a certain manner. Using just a little imagination, you notice the trees printed on the back side look like what appears to be two towers with smoke pouring from them.

The third interesting observation concerning September 11 revolves around the possible birthday of Christ. The traditional day of Christ's birth is celebrated by Christians around the world as December 25. However, from a Hebraic perspective, Christ was more than likely born in or during the seasons of the fall feasts of Israel, namely the Feast of Trumpets, Rosh Hashanah or the Feast of Tabernacles. Some place the birth of Jesus at September 11. I reveal this interesting theory in my book, *Unleashing the Beast*, pages 217 and 218:

> Scholars have placed Christ's birth from as early as 7 B.C., to as late as 1 B.C. No early church source places the birth of Christ before 4 B.C. In fact, Clement of Alexandria, Tertullian, Julius Africanus, Bishop Hippolytus of Rome, Origen and Eueubius all date the birth of Christ between 3 B.C. and 2 B.C. Also, Josephus records an eclipse that occurred at the death of Herod.

Several scholars set the date for the birth of Christ at around September 11 in 3 B.C. The Jewish feast Rosh Hashanah fell on September 11, 3 B.C. Such noted persons as Victor Wierville, author of *Jesus Christ Our Promised Seed*; Craig Chester, co-founder of the Monterey Institute for the Research of Astronomy; and Dr. Ernest Martin, in his book *The Star of Bethlehem: the Star that Astonished the World*, indicate that according to the cosmic signs occurring at that time, September 11 best fits the actual date for the birth of Christ in Bethlehem.

I am certain the terrorists were not aware of this possible link to the birth of Christ, since the majority of Christians are unaware of it as well. Many strange coincidences are related to September 11, but our research must go beyond prophetic sensationalism.

The terrorist attacks had a definite economic, emotional and spiritual impact on the nation. Perhaps our best understanding of the spiritual reasons these attacks fell on our soil may be found in the ancient warnings the Almighty gave to His chosen people, Israel.

The Ancient High Places

The phrase *high places* is recorded 97 times in the English translation of the Bible. This phrase was used to indicate a high location on a hill or a mountain where individuals worshiped an idol or a false God. When Israel repossessed the Promised Land under Joshua, God forbade the Israelites to worship in the high places, and instructed them to destroy the groves and idols the heathen had erected on the hills and mountains (Numbers 33:52).

When Israel failed to destroy the idols and the idolatry surrounding them, God warned that the false Gods would become "scourges in your sides, and thorns in your eyes" (Joshua 23:13). As the years passed, the commitment of God's people to defeat idolatry began to weaken, and they eventually began to mix their religious beliefs with the surrounding heathen tribes and nations. Soon the Hebrew people were joining hands with once-forbidden enemies on the high mountains, worshiping such useless idols as Baal and Ashtaroth (Judges 2:13). When God's chosen people turned to idols, the Bible says, God responded with His own action:

> *And the anger of the Lord was hot against Israel, and he delivered them into the hands of spoilers that spoiled them, and he sold them into the hands of their enemies round about, so that they could not any longer stand before their enemies* (Judges 2:14).

When the Hebrews were plundered by their enemies and taken captive by surrounding nations, they would cry out to

God for deliverance. In His mercy the Lord would bring relief and deliverance to His chosen. This cycle of serving God, turning to idols, going into captivity, crying out to God and being restored back to their land was a continual process in the Old Testament in the time of the judges.

ISRAEL'S SIN	TIME	THE DELIVERER
The groves	**8 years**	*Othniel*, Judges 3:9
Did evil	**18 years**	*Ehud*, Judges 3:15
Did evil	**Unknown**	*Deborah*, Judges 4:2
Did evil	**7 years**	*Gideon*, Judges 6:6
Served idols	**18 years**	*Jephthah*, Judges 10:10

Israel's greatest sin was unbelief. The nation had witnessed the supernatural power of God. After they departed from Egypt, the Almighty opened the Red Sea, brought forth water from a rock, sent manna from heaven for 40 years, cooled the nation with a cloud by day and warmed them with a fire at night (Psalm 78:13-16). Yet, they sinned against God and fell into unbelief. The entire nation wandered through the wilderness for 40 years because of their unbelief (Hebrews 3:8-13).

Later, when they turned to idols God punished the nation by allowing their enemies to invade their land and take the people into captivity. The anger of the Lord was hot against them as they broke their covenant with God:

> *And when the Lord raised up judges for them, the Lord was with the judge and delivered them out of the hand of their enemies all the days of the judge; for the Lord was moved to pity by their groaning because of those who oppressed them and harassed them. And it came to pass, when the judge was dead, that they reverted and behaved more corruptly*

than their fathers, by following other gods, to serve them and bow down to them. They did not cease from their own doings nor from their stubborn way.

Then the anger of the Lord was hot against Israel; and He said, "Because this nation has transgressed My covenant which I commanded their fathers, and has not heeded My voice, I also will no longer drive out before them any of the nations which Joshua left when he died" (Judges 2:18-21).

Israel's idolatry led to God's anger, which eventually brought cycles of God's judgment against the mountains and the high places:

O mountains of Israel, hear the word of the Lord God! Thus says the Lord God to the mountains, to the hills, to the ravines, and to the valleys: "Indeed I, even I, will bring a sword against you, and I will destroy your high places" (Ezekiel 6:3).

This destruction came through a procession of invading armies, storms, earthquakes and numerous other methods that would literally uproot the wooden, clay, brass and stone idols from their resting positions of authority in the high places of the hills and mountains surrounding the cities in the Promised Land.

America's High Places

The United States is a beautiful land consisting of rolling, green hills; deep flowing valleys; rugged mountains; bounding prairies and great plains; and clear blue streams and rivers. At no time in our great history, to my knowledge, have our ancestors ever ascended a high mountain to build a national idol and encouraged or demanded the people throughout the region to worship and bow down to it.

America, however, has prided itself in our national and personal wealth, our stock market and our towering corporate buildings, plazas and enterprises. In our cities are multi-million and, in some cases, multi-billion-dollar glass and steel office complexes from which millions of dollars flow to selective corporations and business markets around the world.

There is certainly nothing wrong with investing money in honest investment opportunities in order to create more wealth. Even Christ gave a parable indicating that people should not become selfish and hide the blessing God has given to His people, but invest the Lord's money and create more money (see Matthew 25:14-27).

However, over the years common citizens have seen investments turn into corporate scandals as CEOs have been overtaken by a spirit of greed. Honest workers have watched their retirement benefits dwindle into oblivion while corporate executives built their multi-million-dollar dream homes. The apostle James gave a last-day warning for the rich who would mistreat their workers:

> *Come now, you rich, weep and howl for your miseries that are coming upon you! Your riches are corrupted, and your garments are moth-eaten. Your gold and silver are corroded, and their corrosion will be a witness against you and will eat your flesh like fire. You have heaped up treasure in the last days. Indeed the wages of the laborers who mowed your fields, which you kept back by fraud, cry out; and the cries of the reapers have reached the ears of the Lord of Sabaoth (James 5:1-4).*

This passage warns that God will judge the wealth of the rich who steal wages from the poor. When greed rules the marketplace and becomes the motivation for working for your wealth and prosperity, then your personal wealth has become your god. By definition, the meaning of *god* in this expression alludes to something a person exalts higher than the true living God of creation. Once an object or a thing is exalted higher than God, it becomes an idol!

Old Testament scriptures use two Hebrew words used for idol. One word is *cemel*, meaning an image or a likeness (2 Chronicles 33:7, 15). Another word is *miphletseth*, which means a "terror; an idol;" and is used in 1 Kings 15:13 and 2 Chronicles 15:16. It is strange that the Hebrew word for *obscene image* or *idol* in 1 Kings 15:13 has the distant meaning of "terror" linked with it.

idolo

Idols themselves often brought a certain fear into the heart of the worshiper. When an idol was worshiped, however, God permitted the people to experience a fear that was not caused by a speechless, lifeless piece of wood or stone. The terror the Lord permitted was to allow armed invaders to sweep through the countryside and seize the possessions of the people, bringing them under subjection and control. This was a fulfillment of a warning given in the Law of Moses:

> *If you despise My statutes, or if your soul abhors My judgments, so that you do not perform all My commandments, but break My covenant, I also will do this to you: I will even appoint terror over you. And I will bring a sword against you that will execute the vengeance of the covenant; when you are gathered together within your cities I will send pestilence among you; and you shall be delivered into the hand of the enemy (Leviticus 26:15, 16, 25).*

Breaking Our Covenant with God

The United States has three main documents that form the foundation of our democracy. They are the Constitution, the Bill of Rights and the Declaration of Independence. The motivation and inspiration behind these documents was the moral and spiritual code of the Holy Bible. Our laws are actually a refined form of several laws and concepts recorded in the Torah (the five books of Moses), the Prophets and the four Gospels.

America's moral laws against murder, incest, sexual perversion, stealing and the like are based on God's laws given to ancient Israel. The moral laws in the Torah formed the written covenant God made with the Hebrew nation, Israel. Their individual and national prosperity depended on their obedience to the written Law of God.

When people followed the commandments of the Almighty, *they were blessed coming in and blessed coming out.* They were made *the head and not the tail, they would lend and not borrow.* No enemy could stand before them in times of war, and their land would produce fruit in its proper season because the rain would come in due season (Deuteronomy 28:1-14).

If, however, they refused to follow the statutes and commandments of God, they would experience drought, famine, lack, sickness, oppression from their enemies and defeat in the time of war (Deuteronomy 28:15-35). For God to allow such negative and painful experiences to come to His "chosen people," doesn't seem fair to the carnal mind. Why would the Lord treat His own people with such strange forms of punishment?

The answer is simple. It only takes one rotten apple to spoil a basket of good apples. The unbelief of ten spies corrupted the entire nation of Israel, causing them to wander in the wilderness for 40 years (Numbers 13). If God allowed a few to worship idols, soon the cancer of idolatry would spread throughout the entire nation. If a handful were permitted to commit adultery and go unpunished, eventually the entire nation would yield to this transgression.

The purpose of the punishments was to expose the reason for the judgment and give the people an opportunity to turn from their ways and return to God. Keep in mind that this life is only a period of perhaps 70 or 80 years, but eternity is forever. God's decisions are always based on eternal principles.

Because America's founding documents are based on the principles of the Biblical Law of Moses, the prophets and the four gospels, then God requires our nation to abide by and live according to the revelation we have in His Word. For many years the Bible was taught in public schools and prayers were offered each morning before classes began. The name of Jesus Christ was revered and treated with respect, and even "sinners" had an inner respect for local churches and ministers.

During these times America grew into a great nation whose ideas of freedom, peace and life impacted the world. As time passed, however, corruption has gradually eaten away at our core values, and our foundation of greatness has been shaken.

Israel's and America's Golden Cow

When God executes judgment on a nation, He judges it by the idols that the nation worships. When God sent the 10 plagues to Egypt, these were not randomly selected pestilences. In Egypt, there was supposedly a major deity worshiped by the Egyptians which should have had the power to control or defeat the 10 plagues. For example, there was a crocodile god linked to the Nile River. There was Ra, a god connected to the sun. There was also a false deity named Apis, a bull, which was worshiped in Memphis, near the land of Goshen where the Hebrews had lived for four centuries. This bull god was linked to the prosperity of the cattle.

When the Almighty sent the plagues to Egypt, He caused the Nile River to turn to blood—and the Nile god was impotent to stop the plague. When the sun was darkened, Ra was powerless; and when the cattle were struck, Apis could not intervene to prevent the death of the cattle in Egypt.

Several days after the Hebrews left Egypt, Moses ascended to the top of Mount Sinai to receive the Ten Commandments. During his 40 days of fasting and prayer, the Hebrews became restless and took their gold earrings and molded a golden calf (Exodus 32:1-4). As they danced and sang to their new god, the calf, Moses returned with the tablets of God's law written by the very finger of the Almighty. In anger, Moses broke the tablets; and in an act of God's judgment, 3,000 Hebrews died at the base of the mountain (Exodus 32:28).

This incident shows that over 400 years of living among the Egyptians in Egypt had deeply influenced the thinking of the Hebrew slaves. God had brought His people out of Egypt, but Egyptian thinking was still in the minds of His people. Building a golden calf may have seemed innocent in the eyes of the people, but it was idolatry in the eyes of God.

The Bull of New York City

New York City is considered to be the chief economic center for the world. The rise and fall of the stock market in New York affects the markets in every nation in the world. The collapse of the stock market in 1929 initiated the Great Depression.

Prior to the Great Depression, a new technology stock was on the rise, called radio. Movies were becoming popular and the word was out that anyone could become rich through investing in the latest technologies.

The years prior to 1929 were called the roaring 20s. America was in a party mood, dancing, drinking, and partying in the big cities. On October 29, 1929, the stock market crashed. More than 15 million shares were traded at a loss of $10 billion. This was twice the amount of currency in the entire United States treasury at the time. The day concluded with some investors committing suicide and others sitting in their offices, penniless and in disbelief.

A prime example is the lives of eight of the wealthiest men of a generation. In 1923, before the Great Depression, these eight men met at the Edgewater Hotel in Chicago to discuss their vast treasures. It was said that they controlled more wealth than the entire U.S. government at the time. Look at what had happened to them just 25 years later:

- The president of the largest independent steel company in the world lived on borrowed money the last five years of his life and died bankrupt.
- The president of North America's largest gas utility company went insane.
- The world's greatest wheat speculator died abroad, insolvent.
- The president of the New York Stock Exchange was sent to Sing Sing Prison.
- A member of the President's cabinet was pardoned from prison so he could die at home.
- The man known as the greatest "bear" on Wall Street committed suicide.
- The President of the Bank of International Settlements committed suicide.

♦ The head of the world's largest monopoly killed himself.

That is how the great stock market crash of 1929 and the Great Depression affected eight of the world's wealthiest men.

Parallels to the 1929 Crash

In the 1990s there was a new family of technology stocks called "Internet stocks." Huge office complexes were erected in Silicon Valley, California, and jobs were abundant in the new Internet business. Popular companies invested millions for online products and Internet services. I was told that thousands of workers purchased new houses, cars, boats and pleasure items with the expectation that the Internet would create billion of dollars in "easy" wealth.

Within a few years these same companies were losing millions, and the effects of unrestrained greed were evident when layoffs began and the large office complexes were placed on the market. Literally hundreds of cars and boats were repossessed and house payments were unable to be paid by thousands of hopeful millionaires.

Israel's golden cow was a form of *Apis*, the god of Egypt; in America, our golden cow of prosperity has been the *stock market*. Ironically, standing just outside the New York Stock Exchange is a brass bull! When the market is creating wealth for investors, it is called a "bull market." I have often said, "If the Almighty refused to allow His chosen people to give honor to a golden calf, He will not permit America to worship at the feet of some man-made brass bull."

Let me assure you that the stock market can be an honest venue to create wealth, if discerned properly. However, it is when greed enters the investor's heart that the motivation of the investor creates his own personal idol. The New Testament warns people of God about being greedy (1 Timothy 3:3 and 3:8). The New Testament Greek word for *greedy* means "to have a desire for gain, especially money or filthy lucre." A Biblical word similar in meaning is the word *covet*. In the Bible, *covet* means "to delight in something to the point of desiring it." In most instances the word has a negative connotation, as in this passage:

You shall not covet your neighbor's house; you shall not covet your neighbor's wife, nor his male servant, nor his female servant, nor his ox, nor his donkey, nor anything that is your neighbor's (Exodus 20:17).

To not covet someone else's possession is the last of the Ten Commandments. Coveting another man's wife resulted in King David having an affair with another man's wife, and setting up her husband to be killed in a battle. He did this to hide the fact that the woman was pregnant with his child (2 Samuel 11). The prophet Micah wrote that when people covet someone's house or property they often attempt to take it by violence and cause oppression against the people (Micah 2:2, 3).

Greed and covetousness causes people to act against others in an inhumane manner. This greed was seen when major executives in leading corporations withheld wealth for themselves and allowed the retirement funds of their workers to be lost.

During the 1990s, America's deity was the brass bull of Wall Street. Investors claimed the bull market would never end; it would only go higher and higher. However, the market bubble, fueled by the Internet and by wild speculation, began to weaken. The market and the power of the bull could not prevent two airplanes from crashing into the towers of the Trade Center, thus creating the greatest assault on American soil since Pearl Harbor. It was also the greatest negative economic recession America had experienced in many years. The fact that the main attack occurred in New York City at the Twin Towers and was carried out by terrorists may not be chance or coincidence.

The Towers in Prophecy

When the Twin Towers collapsed in New York City, numerous scholars searched the scriptures to see if there was a clue or prophetic parallel that gave a prophetic preview to this devastating event. Often when a major, earth-shaking event transpires, a prophetic pattern can be found in the Bible. Research indicated several unusual prophetic passages that took on a new meaning in light of the events of the towers falling. The first was recorded by the Hebrew prophet, Zephaniah:

> *I have cut off the nations: their towers are desolate; I made their streets waste, that none passeth by: their cities are destroyed, so that there is no man, that there is none inhabitant* (Zephaniah 3:6).

Several Bible researchers have noted that the phrase *cut off* means to be destroyed. The prophecy says *nations* will be cut off, and their *towers* (plural) made desolate. The target was the World Trade Center. Offices of over 430 businesses from 26 different countries employed 50,000 people there. The streets surrounding the towers were desolate for days, as business activity came to a halt. Perhaps the most unusual passage that seems to jump from the Scripture was recorded in Isaiah 30:

> *There will be on every high mountain and on every high hill rivers and streams of waters, in the day of the great slaughter, when the towers fall* (Isaiah 30:25).

The passage indicates a great "slaughter," a term used to describe a large number of deaths. Notice that the slaughter occurs the day the towers (plural) fall. There were literally streams of water pouring over the burning ashes from hundreds of fire trucks pouring water on the hot metal beams. Tons of water from broken pipes underneath the towers had to be cleared before rescue efforts could begin.

The Tower of Babel—a Parallel

It seemed the disaster at the Twin Towers painted a picture similar to the famous tower of Babel in Genesis 11. This ancient tower was built by Nimrod, the son of Ham and grandson of Noah (Genesis 10, 11). It represented man's highest accomplishment of global unity. A single language was spoken among the people, and the structure was built high, reaching toward heaven (Genesis 11:4).

The tower was the creation of man's imagination and represented the fact that through human unity nothing is impossible (Genesis 11:6). After carefully examining man's *motive* for erecting the tower, God allowed the man-made tower of Babel to be destroyed. Some Jewish accounts, such as the *Sibylline Oracles*, indicate that a strong wind was sent and caused the brick tower to fall to the ground.

The attack on the Twin Towers was not a direct act of judgment from God, although the terrorists claimed to be acting on God's behalf. The attack arose from the vilest form of human thinking imaginable: a mentality that believes killing innocent people will help one gain favor with God and entrance into some perverted, erotic form of paradise. The attacks, however, could not have occurred without a protective hedge being temporarily removed, such as in the case recorded in Job 1:10-12.

According to the Book of Job the enemy was unable to attack Job, his family or his possessions because of an invisible hedge of protection erected by God (Job 1:10). Only with God's permission and the temporarily removal of the protective hedge was the adversary (Satan) permitted to strike Job's family, destroy and steal his possessions and eventually attack Job's physical body.

In the story of Job, a whirlwind came from the wilderness and "struck the four corners of the house" where his children were gathered. The house collapsed killing all 10 of his children (Job 1:19). Reading this after 9/11, I was struck by the imagery of a strong wind hitting the four corners and the house collapsing killing those inside. I immediately pictured the four corners of the World Trade Center buildings, and how they collapsed, killing those inside, in the same manner Job's children were killed when the four corners of the house fell in on them.

The "whirlwind" in Job was a picture of the storms that arise in the desert, raising swirling dust to where it is impossible to see or breathe. My mind recalled the grey, dusty powder that swirled like a whirlwind through the streets of New York, snuffing out the sunlight and making it almost impossible for people to breathe.

In Job's story, the wind came from the wilderness—the desert area. In fact, Job may have been living in the Middle East, perhaps in the area of Arabia when this story happened. The terrorists were all from the desert lands of Arabia in the Middle East, the same area where Job lived when his attacks came.

Attacks of the Adversary against Job were restrained and limited until the mysterious hedge of protection was removed. Because America was founded by God-fearing people and our documents are based on the Scripture, I believe our nation has been protected by a special invisible hedge that was temporality lifted for a brief season on September 11, 2001. I know that numerous conspiracy theories abound. However, how could 19 hijackers, some on the F.B.I. watch list, get past airport screeners with box cutters and false IDs and hijack four planes at the same time?

It was a well-orchestrated attack and a well-executed one; however, the impact would have been impossible without the invisible hedge of the hand of God being removed, at least for a brief period of time.

God's Personal Terror Warning

A person can read the Bible for many years and pass over important scriptures because at that moment, they do not quicken your spirit. After President George Bush began speaking about a war on terror, I began looking up scriptures that deal with the word *terror*. Having read the Bible through many times, I have read these passages on many occasions. However the word *terror* began to "leap from the pages."

Notice the following predictions and warnings when God's covenant people refuse to obey God's written commandments:

> I also will do this to you: I will even appoint terror over you. . . . . I will set My face against you, and you shall be defeated by your enemies (Leviticus 26:16, 17).

Terror

This scripture is a part of God's warning to Israel about rejecting His Word and His covenant. Notice the terror warning indicates that the Hebrews would be slain before their enemies. When the towers fell, there was rejoicing and dancing in many Islamic countries as satellites began broadcasting the reports and images of slain Americans to the entire world. The Almighty also warned His people that when they grew fat and thick, they forsook God and worshiped new gods (Deuteronomy 32:15-17). He promised that "the sword shall destroy outside; there shall be terror within" (v. 25).

This scripture indicates a two-fold assault of sword without and terror within. In Biblical terminology the phrase *the sword* refers to war. America has been at war in two Islamic nations, Afghanistan and Iraq. We have war without and the threat of terror still lingers within. An entire department called Homeland Security was created by the federal government of the United States to protect the citizens of America from another attack on our soil. For several years, since 9/11, there is still continual concern about another attack which will unfold in the future on the homeland.

Notice that the Lord said, "When you were *fat* you forsook God." The word *fat* alludes to extreme prosperity. It means to shine and to be oily. On many occasions the Lord warned His people to guard themselves against complacency during prosperity. Today we would say, *When you became blessed and prosperous you forsook God.*

During the 1990s, news commentators spoke continually about personal wealth and money and how to get all you can and "can" all you get. When we forsake God, however, we are subject to the same punishments as the ancient people of God. The warnings about terrorism continue:

terrorism

> Your heart will meditate on terror: "Where is the scribe? Where is he who weighs? Where is he who counts the towers"* (Isaiah 33:18)?

Isaiah's prophecy here also alludes to "towers." In Isaiah 33, he speaks of the receiver, or the one who weighs. The Hebrew word means "to suspend or to poise, especially in trade."

To *count* means "to tally or to keep a record." The passage refers to those who keep a record in regard to trade. In this passage a tally is being kept at the towers! Many scholars relegate this prediction to a past fulfillment in ancient Israel. However, some prophecies can have a primary and a secondary meaning. That is, there is a literal fulfillment at a certain moment in Biblical history, and there can also be a secondary meaning that applies to a future, parallel event in prophetic history.

To the question, "Where is the scribe, receiver and he who counted the towers?" the answer is: *They are not found because the towers have fallen and the receivers have been taken out.* While the initial meaning alludes to Israel, the passage seems to have an eerie correlation to the destruction of the towers.

The Number Seven, and the Towers

God warned ancient Israel that if the initial act of judgment did not bring them to full repentance, He would allow them to experience punishment seven times:

> *And after all this, if you do not obey Me, then I will punish you seven times more for your sins* (Leviticus 26:18).

Three times in Leviticus God warns of "seven times" more punishment (see vv. 21, 24). It is interesting to note that the Nazi Holocaust which took the lives of six million Jews, is said to have begun in 1939 and concluded with the Allied invasion and the death of Adolph Hitler in 1945. This seven-year period is identified by some rabbis as the "time of Jacob's trouble" referenced in Jeremiah 30:7.

Traditionally, the time of Jacob's trouble refers to Jacob working seven years to marry Rachel—and was given Leah instead. Jacob worked an additional seven years to finally marry Rachel, the woman he loved (Genesis 29). Laban, the girls' father, told Jacob that in order to marry Rachel he had to "fulfill her week," or work seven more years for Laban (Genesis 29:27). The "seven times more punishment" in Leviticus 26:18 can allude to a seven-year time-frame of punishment, or seven individual punishments. The fact that the Holocaust was seven years in length, presents a strange parallel to this prediction.

Another bizarre twist with the number seven and the collapse of the Twin Towers fascinates me. The entire area where the Twin Towers once stood was identified as the World Trade Center. Each major building was numbered. On September 11, 2001, over 14,000 businesses were affected by the devastation at the site.

- ♦ WTC1 North Tower
- ♦ WTC2 South Tower
- ♦ WTC3 Marriot World Trade Center Hotel
- ♦ WTC4 South Plaza Building
- ♦ WTC5 North Plaza Building
- ♦ WTC6 US Customs House
- ♦ WTC7 World Trade Center

All seven buildings directly connected to the World Trade Center were totally impacted by the attack on September 11. Did the Almighty permit this attack on American soil as a wake-up call for our nation? Is the fact that there are many Biblical prophetic parallels in this attack a warning that we must turn our hearts to God?

In ancient Israel, God permitted famine, war or pestilence to enter the nation in order to gain the attention of His chosen people and turn their hearts back to God. The inspired Scriptures indicate God's favor of blessing, health and prosperity was secured among the Hebrews as long as they faithfully and continually followed God's moral and spiritual instruction. According to former President Harry Truman, America's founding documents—the Constitution, the Bill of Rights and the Declaration of Independence—are based on the Torah (the first five books of Moses), the Book of Isaiah and the four Gospels. We are the only nation on earth whose paper currency is printed with the words, "In God We Trust."

Since Israel and America are spiritually linked through the Word of God and by specific patterns (see our book *Plucking The Eagle's Wings* for amazing detail), then the same blessings promised Israel through the Word are promised to us. The same warnings can be addressed to us and the same judgments can be applied to us.

Terrorism on America's shore is a visible warning that our nation has strayed away from God. We have removed prayer and Bible reading from school, legalized abortion and allowed tax money to pay for it, permitted the gay lifestyle to be accepted and promoted, and we are now allowing the removal of Christian symbols and Christian songs from being sung during holiday seasons. Removing these spiritual landmarks is shoving our unbelief in the face of God.

Will it Happen Again in America?

According to some inside sources there have been seven possible attacks stopped in America since 9/11, and over 70 attacks aborted that were in the planning stages in some form or another. One of the questions often asked is, *Do you believe America will experience another 9/11 form of terrorist attack in the future?* I have posed this question to numerous persons in local, city and federal levels of government.

Those with direct knowledge of counter-terrorism all say they have no doubt that another large-scale attack will unfold in the homeland. It is impossible to guard the borders of Canada and Mexico. If we are unable to stop the flow of illegal immigrants and illegal drugs, how do we think we can stop terrorists from secretly bringing component parts, or chemical and biological weapons across the border?

Some in the Justice Department have said they believe there may be as many as 5,000 possible terrorists in America now. The individuals may not be linked to one another, but all are organized in small "sleeper cells," awaiting the proper signal to strike. Friends in law enforcement in my own community have shared with me that large sums of money were confiscated along the interstate on two different occasions. It was being transferred to Islamic organizations with terrorist links in Florida and New York.

To understand why some Muslims have such a desire to use terror as a weapon, we must understand that Muslims have a large body of prophecies of their own. They strongly believe these prophecies will be fulfilled in the future. A select group of highly motivated Muslims will, on their own accord, help to bring to pass as many of these predictions as possible.

Then the beast was captured and ... the false prophet who worked signs in his presence, by which he deceived those who ... worshiped his image (Revelation 19:20).

2

Unusual Prophecies of the Muslims

Before 9/11, few Americans had understanding or knowledge of the Islamic religion. In fact, most secular Americans couldn't care less about what a Muslim believed. The average citizen thought Islam was an ancient religion formed by a nomad who resided in the Arabian Desert. Most who knew Muslims in America, knew them to be rather quiet, reserved people who more or less minded their own business and seldom fellowshiped outside their religious or ethnic circles.

The suicide bombings of the U.S. Embassies in Kenya and Tanzania, Africa, and the suicide bombing of the guided missile destroyer, USS *Cole*, brought Islam under a universal magnifying glass. The gaping hole at the World Trade Center complex and the burning embers at the Pentagon caused the average American to freshly review the Islamic religion and ask many questions, not the least of which was, "How could anyone, in the name of God (Allah), do something like this?"

Apocalyptic Muslims

It may come as a surprise to learn that most Muslims are interested in the future and have a detailed list of signs that indicate the last days. Many are also highly interested in what the prophets of the Bible say concerning the time of the end.

This is because Islam recognizes many of the Biblical characters, such as Moses, David and Jesus, as prophets. In the Qur'an, Mohammad used stories from the Torah (the first five books of the Bible, written by Moses), and at times even quotes from it, as well as the Psalms and the Gospels.

The Qur'an itself does not contain many predictions concerning the future. However, Muslims also have a series of writings collected in one book called the Hadith. The Hadith is a collection of early Muslim traditions in which many personal friends and contemporaries of Mohammad recall various things they saw him do and statements they remembered hearing him make. Among the various hadith are numerous predictions that relate to the end of days.

When terrorists converted airplanes into flying missiles to strike the Twin Towers and the Pentagon, few Americans realized the prophetic importance of the use of planes in the attack. Not only was this idea important to produce mass casualties, but the motivation for such may have come from a statement found in the hadith, and related by Abdu'r Razzaq:

> Woe to the Arabs because of an evil which has drawn near. Wings! What wings! Long woe in the wings that have a wind in which they move . . .

generated by their movement and [with] a wind emerging from both sides of their movement.

For many years Arab nations have complained about America's use of military technology, especially fighter planes carrying missiles. Palestinians living in the Gaza Strip and the West Bank have pointed out for years that helicopters used to fly missiles into the homes of suspected terrorists were made in the United States.

Some suggest that this passage predicts how the Arabs will be impacted by airplanes. One possible reason the terrorists who struck America used airplanes was to retaliate for the United States assisting Israel in the five wars they have fought with their Arab neighbors. The United States provided military equipment.

According to an inside source who was at the Pentagon during the investigation of the plane crashing into the building, government personnel discovered the body of one of the terrorists who had flown the plane into the Pentagon. He was charred and dismembered, with a portion of his body still strapped in his seat. Before he crashed the plane he had covered himself in some type of shroud whose remains were later identified as an Islamic burial shroud.

A government agent familiar with Islam stated that this man was an "Apocalyptic Muslim." This term is not an Islamic term, but a western religious identification. *Apocalyptic* is a term identifying a belief in the last days, or the end of the world.

An Apocalyptic Muslim is a Muslim who not only believes— as do all practicing Muslims—in the signs of the last days, but is one who is convinced they are obligated to help the Islamic prophecies be fulfilled. They want to see the time of the end of the world come to pass.

Various reasons are given as to why America was attacked. Many commentators point out Muslims' disagreement with America's policy in the Middle East. This is a politically correct way of saying, "They despise America because America supports the Jews and supports Israel." When Americans travel to moderate Muslim countries they are often surprised to see how friendly many of the Muslims are, especially in the more contemporary Muslim countries.

That is, until an American begins to speak positively about Israel. In every Islamic nation of the world, there is an inbred hatred for the Jews and for Israel. Many Muslims enjoy friendship with Americans; but in reality, almost 99 percent do not like the Jews or the fact that Israel exists. This is because of statements made in their sacred books, the Qur'an and the Hadith.

Hating the Jews

During the early days of Mohammad, he said several rather positive things about Jews. In the Qur'an he taught that:

- Israel was God's chosen people (2:47).
- God protected them when they lived in foreign lands (28:4-6).
- Allah (God) would be good to Christians and Jews who believed in one God and performed good works (2:62, 5:69).

As the years passed, however, the Jews rejected Mohammad's claim as a prophet from God. As this rejection increased, Mohammad's hatred for the Jews can be seen in his words that were penned in the Qur'an many years after Mohammad's death. According to the Qur'an:

- Allah turned the Jews into monkeys and pigs because of their wrongdoings (7:166; 5:60; 2:65).
- The Jews changed the Scriptures (7:25; 5:13).
- The Jews are the greatest enemies of the Muslims (5:82).
- The Jews are responsible for wars and trouble (5:64).

Several Muslims have related to me that a common reason for such hatred of the Jews concerns a famous story of how a Jewish woman named Zaineb prepared a lamb on a barbecue for Mohammand and a friend. According to the story, the woman poisoned the lamb, placing extra poison on the shoulder of the lamb, Mohammad's favorite part. When Mohammad bit into the lamb, the story goes, he tasted something strange and took it out of his mouth. His friend proceeded to eat the lamb, however, and later died from the poison.

Muslims say the poisoned meat affected Mohammad's stomach the remaining part of his life. On his deathbed, Mohammad told the sister of his friend who died, "O Ombasheer, what you see in me now (this sickness) is the result of my eating from the lamb that I ate with your brother."

The story of the Jewish woman poisoning Mohammad is told on a continual basis to all Muslims around the world in order to demonstrate how the Jews not only rejected their own prophets which were sent by God to give them "the Book" (the Bible), but how the Jews also rejected, according to Muslims, God's final prophet. Such stories told in Islamic schools only incite more hatred for the Jews.

Many Muslims see Great Britain and America as the two powers that helped create the modern nation of Israel. Muslims note that they built two mosques on the Temple Mount and had control of the city before the Jews took control of the land in 1948. Muslims do not believe, as the Bible teaches, that the Jews had control of the land long before the formation of the Islamic religion.

Because Christians in America accept the same holy book as the Jews (the Bible), Muslims despise America's support for Israel. Muslims have told me, "If America and Britain had not supported the establishing of Israel, the Jews and Israel would not exist today." Many believe that America's connection to Israel was the root cause of the attacks on 9/11.

Others have a rather detailed conspiracy theory that Osama bin Laden was promised oil revenue money if he and his fighters could keep Russia from taking over Afghanistan. Osama and his Mujahadeen (young Jihad fighters) restrained and resisted the Soviet armies by riding horses across the mountains and using weapons provided by Britain and America. After the war, it is alleged, the energy company that was to have passed oil royalties to Osama, sold to another company and the royalty deal was called off.

A friend from Pakistan told me that Osama informed those involved that America would one day pay for not keeping its word and providing him with the money he believed he would receive. This alleged theory forms an interesting conspiracy theory as to the motivation of Osama's attacks.

There may be, however, a "prophetic" reason America was attacked on 9/11. The motivation may be an attempt by Islamic fanatics to help fulfill numerous Islamic prophecies concerning the last days. Muslims have a series of predictions or prophecies, which are said to be signs of the last days. When these prophecies begin to come to pass, they say, it is an indicator that the world will soon come to an end and the final

Islamic teacher, al Mahdi, will rise to power, converting the world to Islam.

Islamic Prophecies— the Sun in the West

One of the final statements Mohammad made before his death involved the west. He said that the sun would rise in the west. This statement has been interpreted in various ways.

Some Islamic leaders, such as Louis Farrakhan, have quoted this passage and given it a self-interpretation. Mr. Farrakhan has implied the "sun" is a great enlightened Islamic leader, such as himself, who will bring the light of Islam to the west, namely the United States. A Muslim friend of mine living in Israel believes this is a supernatural sign of the sun literally rising in the west instead of the east.

A third interpretation is that Islam will eventually take over the west, namely the United States. The fanatics believe this could be accomplished by America submitting or capitulating through terrorism or international blackmail. This form of blackmail was successful in Spain.

Prior to the Spanish elections in March 2004, Islamic terrorists linked to al Qaeda detonated a series of bombs on a major train line in Madrid. At least 192 people were killed and more than 1,400 were wounded. Most of the Spanish population are unaware that Spain is a target, according to Islamic predictions. It is believed that Muslims will take over Spain in the future, through population control and through war.

Many people in Europe are privately becoming concerned about the rise of Islam on the continent. This is one reason that the EU (European Union) has not invited Turkey into their coalition. The EU has one passport and open borders. There is a fear, although not addressed in public, that opening Turkey's borders into Europe will release a tide of millions of Muslims to eventually settle in Europe. This will fulfill their long desire to see the continent that once was the heart of the Roman Empire, come under the political and spiritual dominion of Islam.

It was sad to see the population in Spain vote out a leader who was fighting terrorism in Iraq for a leader who spoke against the war. Because the vote in Spain's election was impacted by a terror attack, Osama bin Laden assumed it would work on the American public. About four days before the presidential election in the United States, Arabic television aired a long speech by Osama, in which he blamed the problems of the world on President George W. Bush.

Osama implied that the re-election of Bush would bring more terror attacks to America, and that any state that voted for Bush would be a special target. Much to Osama's dismay, the video actually backfired against him and Bush won the election by a majority of both popular and electoral votes.

Vote Him Out

A missionary friend traveled to Indonesia just after the presidential election of 2004. He learned that the son of one of the leading terrorist leaders in that Asian nation had received Christ. The young man was in hiding in another location in the nation because of threats on his life. His father, a terrorist who trains men for Jihad, including how to make explosives, placed his own son on a death list!

The young man told the church leaders in Indonesia that before the American election, all the Jihadist were praying to

Allah that Bush's opponent would win. According to his statement they believed that the Democrats would remove the American troops from Afghanistan and Pakistan. From the statements their candidate was making, they perceived he was against the war. Any removal of troops would mean the fanatics could soon make their way back into their strongholds.

Prior to the election of 2004, the Ayatollah Khamenei was quoted: "Everything should be done to ensure the victory of the Democrat candidate in the United States presidential election in November." This comment, as well as the feelings of the leading Jihadists in Indonesia, should make the average American concerned about who we have in public office. When the terrorists see us as weak, we have already lost the war.

When Bush was re-elected, the young Indonesian man said his own father sent out the word that the Jihadist should make plans to do what they can while they can. With Bush in office, they felt, they could all end up dead before he leaves office! While many do not agree with all of Bush's decisions, one must acknowledge he has his pulse on the war on terror, and he understands the dangers to the future of the homeland.

A Great War is Predicted

War and fighting is a central theme in the Qur'an. According to Don Richardson in his book *Secrets of the Koran*, there are 109 identifiable war verses in the Qur'an. This means that one of every 55 verses in the Qur'an is a war verse.

One of Islam's predictions is that there will be a great war between the east and the west. The west will be defeated and the east will rise under the dominion of the Islamic religion. Fanatical Muslims realize that America cannot, at this point in history, be defeated by conventional military might.

America has the greatest fighting force, armed with the latest weapons and most advanced technology in the world. However, they have witnessed the vulnerability of millions of innocent men, women and children who have fallen in their attacks on United States soil.

The attack on America has brought the west into a war in the east (Afghanistan and Iraq), and has created the prophetic scenario that many apocalyptic Muslims have anticipated for centuries. There is, however, one major problem. In the Islamic scenario the west should be defeated and submit to Islam. The opposite is occurring in both Afghanistan and in Iraq.

According to Muslims I have discussed this with, there is a rift among many in the Islamic world as to why the United States is so successful when the Qur'an teaches that Allah (God) will be with the Muslim when he goes into battle. American and allied forces have defeated terrorists in several nations of the world and helped create an atmosphere for democracy in several Islamic nations.

The confusion stems from the ideology that America is an "infidel nation," and according to Iranian Shiite leaders, America is the "Great Satan." Yet, America, this nation of so-called "infidels and devils," is able to defeat its enemies and is given unrestrained access to ferry troops in and out of Saudi Arabia, Afghanistan and Iraq.

Many apocalyptic Muslims, as well as common Muslims, are accepting the fact that America is presently on Islamic soil and occupying these nations. They also believe that the signs indicate something else. They believe that in the near future the final Islamic leader will appear on the world scene and head up a new Islamic coalition that will defeat Israel, the Jews, the Christians and America.

Special Cosmic Signs

In Luke 21:11, Jesus predicted there would be great and fearful signs from the heavens prior to His return. These will include strange signs in the sun, moon and stars (Luke 21:25).

For centuries Christian students of Bible prophecy have followed times of unusual cosmic activity, beginning with the eyewitness accounts of the Jewish historian, Josephus. He tells of numerous cosmic signs that occurred four years prior to the destruction of the Temple in Jerusalem in 70 A.D.

These signs included a large comet that was seen over the city for about a year, and the strange phenomenon of a sword appearing in the sky over the city. Wise men believed these were warnings of the impending destruction of the holy city. Among those who anticipate the arrival of Islam's Mahdi are those who point out several predictions concerning signs in the heavens that are to occur in the last days.

One hadith teaches that the moon will eclipse twice during Ramadan, Islam's holy month. Muslims believe that Mohammad received the revelation written in the Koran during Ramadan. Another cosmic sign said to be a portent of the arrival of the last days is when "a star with a luminous tail will rise from the east before the Mahdi emerges."

During the late 1990s two events occurred that brought a sense of great anticipation to many Muslims in the Middle East. One was the appearance of a comet that had been hidden and was suddenly revealed in 1993. Called the Hale–Bopp comet, it was 50,000 times brighter than Halley's comet. This comet was visible to the naked eye and was considered a sign to Jews, Christians and Muslims who study the signs of the last days according to their religious traditions.

The comet was last seen in Noah's day, about the time Noah was building the famous Ark. As the large comet appeared, many Muslims remembered the tradition of the star with the long tail. This comet exited the galaxy far from the human eye in 1998. When the month of August fell during the Islamic holy month of Ramadan in 1999, a total solar eclipse occurred that month over the Middle East. Ramadan fell during the month of November in 2004.

It was interesting that Osama bin Laden made a video tape prior to the American presidential election. Why did this terrorist mastermind choose five days before the election to show his face to the world when he had been silent and hidden for so long? The answer may lie in the fact that during Ramadan, which occurred in 2004 during the month of November, two eclipses occurred. The Islamic tradition that two eclipses will occur during Ramadan prior to the appearance of the Mahdi may have given bin Laden the opportunity to send the cryptic message that he was the expected one the Islamic world could look to for guidance.

It does appear the timing of certain events has triggered an apocalyptic interest among Jews, Christians and Muslims. All three groups believe in the last days and in the appearing of a future "Messiah." Thousands of books have been written by Christian authors to reveal Jesus as the Messiah. Jewish rabbis have penned their own books attempting to describe the coming Messiah of Israel and signs of his arrival.

There is however, little understanding among Jews and Christians about the expectations of Muslims concerning the time of the end. Muslim interest in the last days motivates them when these "signs" begin to appear, because they believe the Mahdi, their final enlightened one, will appear.

For false christs and false prophets will rise and show great signs and wonders to deceive (Matthew 24:24).

3

The Mysterious Mahdi, Islam's Messiah

In 1991, Yassir Arafat, the late Palestinian leader, contacted Saddam Hussein, then president of Iraq, and congratulated him for waging war against the United States. He promised a glorious time in the future when he (Arafat) would wave the Palestinian flag over Jerusalem as the capital of the Palestinian state. He also evoked images of the coming Islam messiah, the Mahdi, when he predicted Saddam would ride his white stallion across the Mount of Olives toward the Temple Mount.

We know, of course, what happened to these two blood-thirsty despots. However, this incident does introduce an important part of the Islamic prophecy of the last days.

All Muslims believe in the appearance of a mysterious figure identified as al Mahdi, an enlightened one who will appear at the end of time and lead the world in a revival of Islamic law and Islamic justice. Since the year 2000, Islamic messianic fever has been rising, especially in the Middle East and specifically among those living in Afghanistan, Pakistan, Iraq and Iran. This belief in the final Islamic messiah causes grave concern for many in the western intelligence community. They wonder, *Who is this mysterious person? What do Muslims believe about him?* And especially, *How will his appearing impact the world?*

Muslims base their beliefs on two main books. The main book is the *Qur'an*, a collection of writings ascribed to Mohammad, the founder and prophet of the religion of Islam. The sayings in the Qur'an were compiled after the death of Mohammad, and were originally written in the Arabic language. The second most important book is called the *Hadith*. It contains the statements of people who knew Mohammad personally, and heard his instructions.

These statements include how to pray, how to wash your hands and practical details that are not mentioned in the Qur'an. Muslims believe the Qur'an is God's final Word to mankind and that Mohammad is the final prophet of Allah (God). In the Islamic community, traditions handed down from the beginning of the religion serve as a powerful tool of belief. One of these traditions is the Mahdi.

According to Islamic history, Mohammad had 15-20 wives. One of his Jewish wives (he had at least three) is believed to have poisoned Mohammad. He lived for three more years, but never recovered from the poisoned meat. Mohammad did not name a successor, but his daughter, Fatima, was married to a man named Ali. After Mohammad's death, the Muslims split into two groups—the Sunnis and the Shiites. The Shiites accepted Mohammad's son-in-law, Ali, as the true heir to Mohammad's mantle, while the Sunnis followed Abu Bakr.

Mecca, a city in Saudi Arabia, became the headquarters for both branches of Islam. However, the split in the group eventually led to a religious war among the two, and a geographical division of headquarters. In early Islam, two geographical locations were important. They were Damascus, Syria and Baghdad, Iraq. These areas became the early centers of Islam and the capitals of the two main branches of Islam.

The internal struggle over who inherited the prophet's mantle began immediately. Not only was Ali murdered, but the first 11 leaders (Imams) of the Shiite branch were also murdered by the opposing leaders of the Sunni branch. The 12th caliph, son of the 11th, was taken away and hidden in order to prevent his assassination.

According to the Shiites, it appears that no one is certain what happened to the 12th Imam, since his grave was never discovered. Among many of the Shiites in Iran, the tradition developed that the 12th has been supernaturally preserved in a cave or in the desert, and will be revealed to the world at the end of days.

Both branches teach that the coming Mahdi will be a military commander who will defeat all enemies of Islam, and bring a time of peace (Islamic peace, of course) and prosperity to the world. His followers will enjoy much prosperity, including the abundance of gold, silver and precious stones.

Many Muslims in the Middle East believe the Mahdi may be hiding in a cave, and is being protected by special spirits from being killed. According to Islamic belief, just prior to the emergence of this Islamic prophetic figure, a series of unusual signs will occur. These signs include:

- Two European countries will be attacked (some believe it is Spain and Italy).

- A war between the eastern powers and the western powers will occur.
- The west will be defeated and the eastern powers will rise again.
- Three celestial stars will be aligned on one axis.
- A new star, never seen before, will appear in plain sight.
- There will be a war in Syria and eventually a war between the Arabs and Turkey.

Signs Fulfilled During the Past Several Years

The past several years have seen a rise in Islamic fanaticism. This may be due to two important factors. Many Muslims believe the time for the appearing of the Mahdi and the rise of Islam has now come. Islam entered its 1400th year in 1979, the same year Ayatollah Ruhollah Khomeini and his followers seized the U.S. Embassy in Iran and held the workers prisoners for 444 days.

Observers who have studied the Ayatollah's public speeches and his disposition, believe he was attempting to position himself as the Mahdi. Other Islamic leaders point out that Islam is presently in its 40th generation.

Sheikh Nazim Adil al-Haqqani, an international Muslim cleric, declares he met the 39th sheik in the "Golden Chain" that began with the prophet Mohammad in Damascus over 50 years ago. But this Golden Chain is not presently in its 40th generation, according to the sheik. Leaders like him are teaching that the Mahdi will be a part of the line of the 40th generation.

Others, such as his majesty King Hussein, the former King of Jordan, was said to be the 43rd generation from Mohammad. Either way, these numbers are important to those studying Islamic messianic expectations. There is a fresh stirring in many Islamic circles that the day of Islam becoming the world's greatest power is upon us. As one noted cleric said, "The 21st century will be the century for Islam."

Sheikh Nazim Adil al-Haqqani says, "We know that this world is being prepared for huge appearances. All nations and all mankind are being prepared for something that is approaching soon. These are huge events, unexpected huge events." Recent events add fuel to his suppositions. The fact that Osama bin Laden was able to attack the greatest military power on earth from a cave and impact the economy of millions, is considered a supernatural feat and a sign to Muslim extremists that the great day is upon them.

In November of 2003, during the Islamic fast in the month of Ramadan, Muslim scholars noted that three stars were aligned. This caused quite a sensation throughout Europe and the Middle East. Another "sign" occurred on March 15th, 2004 when the media reported that a distant unknown galaxy with new stars had been discovered. Islamic web sites were filled with optimism that these cosmic signs were given to encourage Muslims not to give up their hope of eventually dominating the world.

During a series of raids in Afghanistan, the U.S. military seized a videotape in which bin Laden was teaching. He was using a dry-erase board on which he had written the Arabic phrase, "awaited enlightened one." Experts believe bin Laden was attempting to make a connection between himself and the awaited Mahdi, and perhaps was claiming the ancient "prophecy" for himself.

According to various intelligence sources, interrogators at Guantanamo Bay have said that some detainees joined bin Laden's terrorist network because of their belief that he was the "awaited one." Terrorists from several Islamic nations, including Iran and Syria, are crossing over into Iraq. Their inspiration is drawn from the belief that the Mahdi will soon appear in Iraq!

One tradition is that the Mahdi will have the same name as Mohammad. Since the end of 2001, bin Laden has been signing his name "Osama bin Muhammad bin Laden." It is clear that Osama is playing on the Islamic expectations of the coming al Mahdi, and attempting to plant the seed into the minds of simple Muslims that he, Osama, is that one whom the entire Islamic world is expecting. He will be a legend to Extremist Muslims when he is eventually captured or killed.

This tradition is so inbred that after the initial ground war in Iraq, an Islamic leader from the city of Fallujah formed the Mahdi army, a small band of highly inspired rebels numbering up to 8,000, who resisted the American troops for several weeks and demanded that Americans pull out of Iraq.

The Black Banners

In June, 2003, Muqtada al-Sadr, a radical Muslim religious leader and Shiite cleric, created a militia force in Iraq. This was shortly after America invaded Iraq and had begun to organize a temporary form of government. This religious leader began calling his militia the "Mahdi Army." I know of no news organization or commentator that even attempted to explain why this religious zealot used the phase, "Mahdi Army." It is clear, however, that al-Sadr is very familiar with the Islamic prophecies involving the belief that the Mahdi will arise out of

Iraq. Along with those imams ruling in Iran, he is often seen wearing a black turban.

Once again if we turn to the hadith where Thawban reported that the "Messenger of Allah, bless him and peace be upon him, said, 'When you see the black banners coming from Khurasan, then go to them, even if it means crawling over the snow. The Deputy of Allah, the Mahdi, will be among them.'" It is also reported that Mohammad said, "The black banners will come from the east and their hearts will be as firm as iron."

According to Muslims I have spoken with, many of the Iranians believe they are the fulfillment of this prophecy—they are the people from the east whose hearts are as firm as iron. Another hadith states that the black banners will go to war and emerge as the winners. In the minds of Shiite Muslims, especially those living in Iran, they will fulfill this prediction. Terrorism is the key to their future success.

In July 2005, nine men on trial in Amman, Jordan, confessed to plotting to unleash a deadly cloud of chemicals in the heart of Amman. Their targets included the U.S. Embassy, the Jordanian prime minister's office and the headquarters of Jordanian intelligence, but the blast and toxic cloud would also have completely destroyed a large medical center, a shopping mall and a residential area. The terrorists admitted their goal was to kill 80,000 people.

> Jordanian authorities said the attack would have mixed a combination of 71 lethal chemicals, which they said has never been done before, including blistering agents to cause third-degree burns, nerve gas and choking agents.
>
> A Jordanian government scientist said the plot had been carefully worked out, with just the right amount of explosives to spread the deadly cloud without

diminishing the effects of the chemicals. The blast would not burn up the poisonous chemicals but instead produce a toxic cloud, the scientist said, possibly spreading for a mile, maybe more.

"Our Sheikh Abu Musaab al-Zarqawi said that if we had chemical weapons we would have hit Tel Aviv *and* the Jordanian regime," the *al-Hayat Daily* quoted Hussein Sharif as saying in his confession. Zarqawi is the head of al Qaeda in Iraq and is under indictment by the United States. He lived for awhile in Iran and worked for the Iranian government.

Iran Hotspot

During his State of the Union address in 2002, President Bush announced that three nations, Iraq, Iran and North Korea, were an axis of evil. The usual talking heads of political commentary analyzed the remarks and criticized Bush for making such statements and leveling wild conjectures against these three nations.

As time passed, the journalists were proven wrong and the President was proven correct. These three nations were a trio of reckless fanaticism and dictatorships fueled by anti-western propaganda.

First was Iraq. While the reports from government sources have said that Saddam did not have weapons of mass destruction in Iraq, those inside countries such as Iran and Syria seem to know where these "invisible" parts, components and weapons are located. A Syrian journalist, dying with cancer, moved to France just after the intense fighting and began to tell how Saddam moved his important materials into Syria prior to the war. He said some of the material was placed in caves in remote areas near the border.

One report said that over 40 trucks, amassed at the border of Iraq and Syria several days before the war, were moving materials out of the country prior to the initial attack from the coalition forces.

According to a leak from Iran, a military leader in Iran said some of Saddam's dangerous weapons were hidden deep in the earth, near a small airport in Iraq. This is very logical, since Saddam was personally terrified of any chemical or biological weapons. The coalition forces moved through buildings, warehouses and some underground bunkers and discovered no weapons of mass destruction. The most deadly of Saddam's arsenal could have been hidden away from a major city, however.

It is known that the Chinese and German engineers made plans and assisted in building several major tunnels and bunkers for Saddam. Iraqis who assisted in the effort to provide Saddam's hiding places, were often killed after the project was completed to avoid them ever telling where the dictator's secret chambers were located.

Some have suggested that the chemicals meant to create a toxic cloud over Amman, Jordan, in 2004, were a part of Saddam's arsenal. It is known that they were hauled into Jordan from Syria.

The subject of North Korea is still being written, and the greatest fear is that the dictator there will build nuclear weapons and sell them to Islamic fanatics, or will continue to build nuclear bombs that can be used against the west.

The real threat, however, is Iran. Islamic religious leaders control the government, and they are classified as radical and fanatical in their Islamic interpretations of the Qur'an and the Hadith. Iran has the strongest belief and anticipation of the coming Mahdi. It is the Iranian version of the Mahdi that contains the doctrine of the 12th Imam, the son of the 11th, who was hidden and will reappear at the end of days. This 12th Imam may play a role in a future attack on America.

The 12th Imam Operation

The Iranian government is known to host terrorists and sponsor insurgencies in Iraq. It hopes to eventually overtake Iraq, once America and the coalition are gone. Iranian defectors claim Osama bin Laden has entered the country on several occasions. He was even given refuge in a safe house in the northern part of the country.

This same information was also related to me by a man from Iran, who said the common people in Iran know the government is in contact with the terrorist mastermind. Iranian leaders have an innate fear that either Israel or America will eventually conduct a military operation to stop Iran from developing nuclear weapons that will be used in the future against Israel and the West.

Motivated by this fear, it is believed that certain Iranian leaders are secretly preparing to retaliate against the United States by setting up sleeper cells and getting deadly materials into their hands. A major attack in the United States may be credited to the Mahdi.

Congressman Curt Weldon, a special agent who retrieved information from inside the Iranian government, has written an excellent book, *Countdown to Terror*. In it he says there is a planned attack on the United States called "The 12th Imam Operation." This 12th Imam refers to the famous Mahdi of Islam, who is expected to appear, convert the whole world, then kill the Jews and Christians who reject Islam.

Ayatollah Ali Khamenei, Iran's Supreme Commander, is an Islamic religious leader who is also the country's leading political power. According to the Iranian Constitution, he will be the Supreme Commander "until the reappearance of the 12th Imam." Inside sources say that Khamenei claimed the 12th Imam appeared to him in a dream and told him to plan an attack against America!

According to Congressman Weldon, in a private meeting of nine major Iranian officials, Khamenei told the officials he believed the United States or Israel would eventually attack Iran. On April 18, 2003, he announced publicly that Iran is preparing for this assault.

He allegedly announced in the private meeting that there were seven members of al-Qaeda in Canada and the United States who already have chemical and biological products. The leader stated that these seven would be provided with chemical and biological products from Iran, and they would retaliate if Iran was attacked.

Whatever their future plans, these small al-Qaeda groups and individuals who are brainwashed into the terrorist way of thinking, want the next attack to be more spectacular and more deadly than 9/11. No doubt, one strategy involves some form of chemical, biological nuclear or dirty)bomb that will be detonated over a major American city. I would not be surprised if as many as five locations were targeted coordinated explosions of disaster.

The London Bombing

The underground subway in London was attacked by Islamic terrorists. Days later, several bombs were discovered that had not exploded. Evidence indicated that a second wave of planned attacks had failed. The motive given for the attacks was that the young Muslim men disagreed with the government about the war in Iraq and about Muslims dying throughout the world as a result of the war on terrorism.

With attacks in America, Spain and London; and with the deaths of many Australians in Bali bombing in Indonesia, people are asking, "Should we pull our military forces out of Iraq? Was it worth going to war in Iraq? Should coalition forces have allowed Saddam to continue ruling under the United Nations oversight?"

What America Did Not Realize

Was invading Iraq the right thing to do? Absolutely! Saddam Hussein had used poison gas on the Kurdish population in his own country, killing thousands. He not only invaded Kuwait, setting over 500 oil wells on fire, he also had hundreds of thousands of Muslims murdered. He and his two sons tortured countless others for their own twisted pleasure.

Evidence is mounting that Saddam had close links to al-Qaeda and was planning on developing deadly WMDs that, within a few years, would be given to terrorists to attack key targets in Europe and America. Saddam's two sons, Uday and Qusay, were demons clothed in human flesh.

On one occasion, according to a bishop from Iraq, Uday drove up to a public restaurant, spotted a young Christian girl, entered the facility, raped the girl in front of her parents, then shot her and her family in cold blood. For those who say the war wasn't worth it: Was the war with Germany and the removal of Hitler worth the effort? Ask the Jews! Was the removal of Saddam worth the effort? Ask the persecuted Iraqis!

American military leaders were told by Iraqi defectors that when Iraq was liberated, the Americans would be considered as heroes and liberators. The impression was that democracy was desired and that after the removal of Saddam, peace would follow. This is not what occurred.

The main reason there has not been peace is that Iraq is a nation consisting of three different groups of Muslims: the Kurds in the north, the Shiite in the south and the Sunni Muslims in the central part of the country. The Sunni and Shiite have fought each other during 14 centuries; and throughout Islamic history Iraq was a center of the conflict.

Plans to Hurt the American Economy

With a crackdown on illegal immigration, the new laws for entering and exiting the country and the new Patriot Acts, it has become more difficult for Islamic fanatics to hide within America and escape detection or observation.

The propaganda war is difficult for America to win, however, especially when the Islamic governments own the television and satellite stations in the Middle East and in parts of Europe. This propaganda battle takes on strange forms at times.

The Coca-Cola® Scare

Some time back, a member of my staff spoke to a woman from South Carolina who was warned to avoid all Coca-Cola® products outside of a grocery store by a man who appeared to be from the Middle East. I learned later that the same "warning" was given out in Florida, Tennessee and Alabama by individuals who appeared to be Middle Eastern, but out of "concern," were repeating a warning they had "received."

A short time later I contacted a friend in the Justice Department in Washington and told them about these series of warnings that were coming to my attention. They called the man on my staff to personally get more information. After a detailed investigation, the following information was discovered.

A Muslim businessman in France had developed a new soft drink, a cola called Mecca Cola. It was supposed to be similar to the traditional Coca-Cola®. However, when a person purchased Mecca Cola, a portion of the proceeds went to support the Muslim religion. There are six million Muslims in France, and the businessman saw an opportunity to both sell a product that was not from America and in return, the Islamic religion would gain a commission.

It is believed that someone linked to supporting the new Mecca Cola attempted to plant the false idea that somehow the Coke® in America was being tainted and could be dangerous to consumers. If the rumor would spread to enough people and the national media picked up on the warning, then Coke® products in America could suffer, and this would work well for the new Mecca Cola in France. The entire scare was a hoax that failed.

There are, however, other areas in which some Muslims may be attempting to hurt the economy of the United States. Three areas are:

- The changing of dollars to Euros
- The future oil crisis
- The hoarding of gold

Exchanging Dollars to Euros

The European Union (EU) introduced the euro currency several years ago. It is now common for the euro to maintain an equal or higher value than the dollar. The British use the pound; the Japanese, the yen; and the Americans, the dollar. For years the nations of the world desired to have hard currency in hand and the dollar was the premium currency.

I recall visiting Bulgaria and Romania after the fall of Communism. In Romania one American dollar was equivalent to 600 Romanian dollars. A beautiful men's suit could be purchased for $20. A full-length mink coat that would sell for $6,000 in the United States could be bought there for $400 American dollars. The same is true in many third-world countries. Since World War II, the dollar has sustained its buying power in the nations of the world. However, the euro has now changed the equation.

From time to time the euro has been a desired investment and currency in much of Europe. It appears that Muslims angry at America for going to Afghanistan and Iraq are now spreading the word that Muslim nations should avoid using dollars and begin using euros as their international currency. While the change is difficult for many, because some of the Arab leaders have huge amounts of cash in American dollars stored away in secret vaults, the rising tide of voices against the American dollar are increasing in volume.

The Future Oil Crisis

Many remember the oil embargo from the early 1970s. American weapons had assisted the Israeli military in defeating the Syrian army in the 1973 Yom Kippur War. With the assistance of Britain and American technology, the young, reborn Jewish nation was spared a terrible nightmare and possible devastation. To protest our support, OPEC (the oil-producing nations), under pressure from Saudi Arabia, began an embargo on the oil coming to the west, especially from the Arabian Peninsula.

The U.S. government expected long fuel lines and gas shortages. Fuel prices jumped to a then stunning $1.25 a gallon in many cities. You could purchase gas on an even-numbered day if the last number on your car tag was an even number. Odd numbers permitted gas purchases on odd-numbered days. My father pastored in Arlington, Virginia (near Washington D.C.), and the gas lines were very long and the patience of the drivers very short!

Within months the crisis was settled and the black liquid gold from the sands of Arabia began to pump out of the earth. At times the relationship between the United States and Saudi Arabia has been stretched, but nothing can compare to the stress that came after 9/11.

After the attacks on the World Trade Center and the Pentagon, it was discovered that the 19 hijackers were Sunni Muslims, not the expected Shiite radicals. Intelligence sources also learned that the suicide teams were Saudi Arabian. I was informed by a Pakistani Christian that there may have been up to 80 Muslim men from the Gulf Region training to be pilots in American flight schools. Some may have had a legitimate cause, but others may have been planning future attacks using airplanes.

This is one of the reasons some of the flights from Europe were kept from entering America. Some sources believed that some of the Muslim pilots were sympathetic to the causes of certain radical groups, and when various combinations of names showed up on the airline manifest, the flight was cancelled.

The stress between America and Saudi Arabia (who allegedly helps fund some terror activity) is at an all-time high. The Saudis understand that without the military support and intelligence information from the Americans, the Royal Family is in grave danger of possible assassination attempts. I have spoken with individuals who have worked in Saudi Arabia, and they tell me the poor and common people in Arabia and in the surrounding Gulf States despise the wealth and the lifestyle of the Royals in Arabia. For this reason, Arabia needs America's support.

However, America is still dependent on Saudi oil (40 percent of our imports are from the Middle East). While a greater percentage of our imports are purchased from other nations, we are still in need of the Saudis' oil favors. The danger of this dependence cannot be overstated.

What if a fanatical regime seized control of the oil wells in Saudi Arabia? America would be brought under subjection to the desires of a few and the nation would enter a time of economic panic. Fuel prices would soar, halting the delivery of goods and services. Within a few months, major truck lines would be out of business and the airline industry would be in total bankruptcy.

Pockets of fanatics presently believe that this is the jugular vein in the neck of the United States. We must have oil and gas or the economy stops. We should be drilling for oil in Alaska and off the coasts of Mexico right now. We should be building several new refineries, because it takes years to pump the oil from the ground and years to complete a refinery. May I suggest that if the House of Representatives and the Senate continue to refuse to drill in America, they will discover one day that their limousines are on empty!

The future oil crisis is alluded to in Daniel. The future Antichrist of Bible prophecy will control the "fattest places of the province" (Daniel 11:24). The root word for *fattest* is the word for oil. The word for "province" is the word *medina*. How strange that Medina is the place where Mohammad is buried in Saudi Arabia, and Saudi Arabia makes its billions in oil!

The Hoarding of Gold

Gold is very important to Islamic apocalyptic tradition. The Hadith mentions a statement that someone overheard Mohammad make:

> *He heard the Messenger of Allah say: "A time is certainly coming over mankind in which there will be nothing (left) which will be of use save the dinar"* (Imam Ahmad ibn Hanbal).

In early Islamic history a gold coin was minted called the *dinar*. After the collapse of the Ottoman Turkish Empire in 1924, there was a lapse in the Islamic currency when most Muslim countries accepted the currency of the western nations, including the British pound and the American dollar. Several years ago an Islamic group in West Malaysia began minting a new gold dinar.

Meetings have been conducted in Egypt and in Arabia, discussing the need for Muslims to accept the new coinage as the official coin of the Islamic nations. In brief, many apocalyptic Muslims with traditions concerning the last days believe there will be a worldwide economic crisis in which all paper money will be useless. The only money of value will be money consisting of gold and silver.

Many speculate this is one reason gold and silver prices have risen from time to time by 40 or 50 percent in a short time. In early 2003 the price of gold and silver was rising, but after the invasion of Iraq the price increased by about 30 percent! There was no explanation for this because the stock market was rising, the jobless rate was decreasing and the economy was again on the move. The explanation may be found when we explore who is hoarding the gold and silver.

Intelligence research indicates that Muslims are now telling fellow Muslim businessmen to purchase as much gold as possible and get an edge on the market. Huge amounts of gold would provide enough material to produce large numbers of the thin gold dinars. An Islamic banking system could sell these coins to fellow Muslims.

If you think this sounds too far-fetched, remember how silver went to $50 an ounce in the 1980s, and the price of gold peaked at over $800 an ounce. You may recall how one man attempted to get the market on the metals and was stopped by the government. History confirms that when a major economic crisis blankets the world, precious metals, such as gold and silver, are sought after by investors, businessmen and private citizens.

Why Democracy Does Not Work in Muslim Nations

When people from foreign nations immigrate to America, they are overwhelmed by our prosperity and our freedom. Often they are inspired to duplicate this freedom in their home countries. At times, nations such as the former communist-controlled Eastern Europe, successfully take the democratic road and begin a new society based on political and religious freedom.

However, the only true democracy in the Middle East is Israel. The surrounding Islamic nations are all ruled by either a king or a presidential dictator. When America set out to form a democracy in Iraq, they failed to realize that in the eyes of many Muslims, the word *democracy* is related to America, to Christianity or to Israel. In their eyes democracy is not about freedom as much as it is the taking of western ideas and forcing an ancient culture to follow the same path as the United States.

When these nations see television programs coming from America, they see drug addiction, alcohol, sex, pornography and rock-and-roll music. This is what the average Muslim thinks America is all about. A true Muslim is taught not to drink alcohol and not to be involved in gambling. The women in some conservative countries are covered from head to foot, and only their eyes peer out of the black veils. The religious leaders reject the notion of a western democracy coming into their country. After all, who wants the drugs, the alcohol and the evils that come with the freedom?

This is one reason the stricter Muslims reject the concept of freedom and democracy. Recently, terror groups warned Iraqis that if democracy came to Iraq, the government would permit gays to marry. This is their concept of American democracy.

A second reason real democracy seems to fail in Islamic-controlled nations is that for true democracy to work, its laws must be based on moral and spiritual principles. Specifically, America's democracy is based on the principles of the Holy Bible. The three main founding documents of the United States—the Constitution, the Declaration of Independence and the Bill of Rights—were written by men who believed in God and Jesus Christ, and who used the Scriptures as their source of moral principles.

When a nation rejects the Holy Bible and the teachings of Moses, the prophets, the Gospels and the revelations of Paul, then there is no true foundation on which to build a democracy.

Political freedom can only be enjoyed when there is true spiritual freedom of the human spirit.

In Afghanistan the Taliban ruled the people with laws called the Sharia, which controlled dress and restricted personal freedom. They allowed no televisions, no radios and no printed materials from the west. This strict Islamic law was considered spiritual freedom from the evils of the world. However, it only led to resentment and bondage.

Those who truly wish to copy the American lifestyle must look beyond the marble halls of Congress to the churches scattered like lighthouses, beaming hope throughout rural America. Our spiritual freedom is the anchor of our political freedom. We believe we are "one nation under God." Our personal relationship with the Almighty creates a love for all of mankind, and a compassion for the poor and needy.

Iraq and Islam's Coming Mahdi

The historic link between Iraq, the early times of the Islamic religion and the expectations of the coming Mahdi cannot be overstated. Iraq is not only a hot spot for present prophetic implications, but it has a long Biblical and secular history. And it has a definite place in prophecy.

Historically, the land known as Iraq was once the global headquarters for the world's first global government. This occurred under the leadership of Nimrod, the son of Cush, the son of Ham (see Genesis 5, 10). The famous Tower of Babel was destroyed by God himself, and the peoples were scattered abroad and their languages confused.

Centuries later, the famous patriarch Abram was called out of the land of Ur (in Iraq) to sojourn in a strange country and form a new nation, Israel. From ancient Babylon (Iraq), three major empires of Bible prophecy have ruled: the Babylonian Empire, the Media-Persian Empire and the Grecian Empire—in that order.

From a purely spiritual standpoint, the region of the world where Iraq sits is also important geographically. Beginning at the Atlantic Ocean, this rectangular-shaped area on the world map stretches across Africa and Asia between 10 degrees and 40 degrees north of the equator. It spans approximately 60 countries, and is the darkest, neediest and most difficult region to reach with the gospel on the face of the earth.

- Two-thirds of the world's population—more than 3.2 billion people—live in the 10/40 Window.

- Of the 400 cities of the world with a population of over a million people, 300 of them lie within the 10/40 Window.

- On a list of the least evangelized mega-cities of the world, the top 50 are in the 10/40 Window.

- More than 97 percent of the poorest of the poor live in the 10/40 Window.

- The average person living in the 10/40 Window exists on less than $500 per year.

- Over 95 percent of the world's unreached people groups—those who have never heard the gospel—live within the 10/40 Window.

- Islam, Buddhism and Hinduism are all centered within the 10/40 Window. Over 71 percent of all Muslims, 98 percent of all Hindus, and 68 percent of all Buddhists live in the 10/40 Window.

- Where these religions are strong, Christianity is often practiced underground or under great persecution.

♦ Iraq is located in the very center of the 10/40 Window.

In my research of the importance of Iraq, I have discovered that many Muslims from the Shiite branches of Islam believe that the Mahdi of Islam will actually emerge from one of two possible locations in Iraq: either from Samarra or from Karbala.

Americans have difficulty understanding how a single nation, Iraq, can have four different groups—the Sunnis, the Shiites, the Kurds and the Christians—who all call themselves Iraqis; yet, inflict such acts of terrorism on each other. I remind my friends that less than 150 years ago America was split between the North and the South in a Civil War. Brother fought against brother and father against son. Entire households were divided over the issue of slavery. Keep in mind that slavery was a social issue, but the war was a social/religious issue. Those who believed in slavery fought against those who resisted slavery.

In Iraq the issue is not just democracy versus Islamic fanatics. The overriding issue is which religious group will retain power and control over the government in the country. Under Saddam Hussein, the Sunni Muslims received the better treatment and the Shiites in certain areas were often tortured and killed. This was because Iran is neighbor to Iraq, and the Iranians are 98 percent Shiite Muslim. Saddam conducted a 10-year war with the Shiites of Iran, and finally called a cease-fire.

When the Shiites made an attempt to oust Saddam after the Gulf War, however, the wrath of the dictator came down on the people who rebelled, as he slew hundreds of thousands of them over a period of time.

There is a strong expectation that Islam's final "awaited one" who will eventually convert the world to the Islamic religion will arise either from Arabia or from Iraq. This is why it is important to keep our attention focused on this region of the world to see what future developments tie in with these Islamic predictions.

If events do not unfold in the manner the apocalyptic Muslims teach, we may see a large group of Muslims assist in the fulfillment of these predictions by "making things happen" that appear to be the fulfillment of these predictions.

These "things" they make happen include acts of terror to bring down certain governments and economies.

It was granted to the one . . . to take peace from the earth, and that people should kill one another, and there was given to him a great sword (Revelation 6:4).

4

How Terrorists Fulfill Biblical Prophecies

When people in the 21st century read certain unusual Biblical prophecies recorded over 2,000 years ago, their first impression is to say, "This passage cannot be fulfilled in our generation." This is especially true concerning prophecies that speak of the war to occur in the last days. An example is found in Ezekiel 38 and 39.

The War of Gog and Magog

One of the better-known future wars recorded in the Bible is found in these chapters. This end-time battle is known as the war of Gog and Magog. In Ezekiel 38:5, 6, the Biblical prophet lists Islamic nations participating in this battle against Israel:

- ♦ Persia
- ♦ Ethiopia

+ Libya
+ Gomer
+ Togarmah, the people from the North Quarters

Today, Persia is the nation of Iran, one of the centers for Islamic fanatics in the Middle East. Ethiopia is a country in the northeastern horn of Africa. It was once a strong Christian nation, but today it is torn apart by Islamic fanatics. Libya is also a Muslim country. Many scholars believe Gomer is the region around Germany. Togarmah encompasses the area of Turkey, Armenia and the southern republics of the former Soviet Union. All of these are north of Israel, and comprise five major Muslim nations.

Fifty years ago the nations listed above had leaders who were pro-western and completely cooperative with the west. Today things have changed and these regions of the world have come under the control of not just Islamic leaders but also the influence of Islamic fanatics. The difficult passage in Ezekiel is where the prophet said that horses would be used during battle:

> Then you will come from your place out of the far north, you and many peoples with you, all of them riding on horses, a great company and a mighty army. You will come up against My people Israel like a cloud, to cover the land. It will be in the latter days that I will bring you against My land (Ezekiel 38:15, 16).

Modern nations do not use horses in battle. Today's military equipment consists of tanks, helicopters and fighter jets. In the future, computers will control the missiles and other weapons of war. Large ships, underground bunkers, and satellites moving thousands of miles above the earth are linked to computers and global positioning equipment. These are the most effective tools in winning a conflict in modern warfare.

Modern scholars who read Ezekiel immediately form opinions. Either this prophecy already happened at some point in history, they say, or the words of the prophet cannot be taken literally because no one uses horses in battle today. Let me answer this criticism.

First, no historical records in Israel's long history indicate this prophecy has already been fulfilled. This war is destined for the latter days (vv. 8 and 16). The term *latter days* is used by the Biblical prophets to indicate the time prior to the return of the Messiah. *Secondly*, to say these words cannot be taken literally has no theological or Biblical basis. **When the plain sense of the Scriptures make sense, then seek no other sense!**

Three possible problems can occur with the modern equipment we use in electronic warfare. First, computer hackers can create havoc on computer codes with EMPs. Viruses can also wipe out vast amounts of vital information. I have been informed that a bomb is being developed that can affect the electrical circuits of computer systems, thus making them ineffective to release information and communicate with other computers.

A second problem concerns satellites overhead. In the future seven-year Tribulation, "the stars will fall from heaven" (Matthew 24:29). This phrase means that large meteorites will rain down on the earth. Several years ago a large meteorite shower occurred that caused great consternation in the United States. Scientists were concerned about space dust from the meteorites affecting the many satellites in the sky.

A large meteorite shower could hit military satellites in the sky and knock them out, thus making any contact with ships and underground facilities difficult, if not impossible. I was also told that if a large missile containing small grains of sand exploded in space, it is believed this would disrupt the satellites.

Fighting on Horses

Recent information makes the concept of fighting the "old-fashioned way" on horseback a stronger possibility than ever. The latest concern by United States intelligence sources is an EMP, or electromagnetic pulse, threat. An EMP attack can be created by detonating a nuclear weapon at altitudes a few miles above the earth's surface. The explosion would create a set of electromagnetic pulses that interact with the earth's atmosphere and the earth's magnetic field.

The results of this attack would be absolutely devastating. The EMP would damage the electrical power systems and all electronics, including computers. Anything requiring the use of electricity would be rendered powerless. The results would include the shutting down of power grids, water plants, banks and a list of other vital agencies needed for daily service and human survival.

During the 2004 season of the popular program *24*, one of the weekly episodes demonstrated the impact of this threat. When the star of the show, Jack Bauer, was investigating the link of a terrorist with a major American company, the head of the company set off a small EMP in order to destroy all information in the offices and erase information showing their link to terrorists. The bomb did not kill anyone, but it shut off all electricity in an eight-mile radius.

In a 2005 meeting in Washington, Senator Jon Kyl and Representative Roscoe Bartlett warned that a small terrorist group with as little as $100,000 could put together one of these bombs and effectively cripple American society and eventually kill millions. The challenge would be getting food and fresh water to the needed places when all communication is shut off.

Remember, in an effective attack there would be no access to television, to the use of your air conditioner or electric heat, to your microwave, to lights in your house or anything else that operates with electricity.

Imagine how a major city would react to an attack from which it could take six months to a year to recover! Several years ago a major snow storm was coming to the state of New York. In the city, people were pouring into grocery stores, filling their carts with food and canned goods. When people saw others with several boxes of their favorite cereal on one shopping cart, fights began to break out. One store clerk actually feared for her life, as people pushed, shoved and demanded their share of the groceries that others had in their carts!

According to some sources, there is a concern that a foreign ship could hover offshore and launch a Scud missile toward one of our major cities and detonate it in the atmosphere. With the proper warhead, it would create the desired effect of an EMP. If this type of attack occurred anywhere in the world, the nation where the EMP strike occurs would have its modern military rendered almost powerless, since most modern nations use computers and electronic devices in their military arsenals.

Could this be why the great war against Israel in Ezekiel 38, 39 mentions the enemy using horses in the battle? I often felt it was because horses would be more mobile in the rugged mountains of the Golan Heights in Israel, and the area near the mountains of Jordan. However, a major EMP attack could change the armies from using computer-controlled weapons relying on hand-to-hand combat with animals as transportation.

Millions of people in Third World countries would not be affected by such an attack, other than any radiation that may spread. This is because they do not depend on computers or electricity. Prior to the year 2000, I was with a missionary friend ministering in a large stadium meeting in Kenya. We were staying at a beautiful hotel, a few miles from the city. Each morning we enjoyed a lovely breakfast with fresh fruit picked from the trees nearby.

One morning I looked out the window and saw the grounds-keepers trimming the edge of the grass with a machete. In America, people were discussing the possible problems of Y2K and a possible major computer glitch. I laughed and told my friend, "The people here won't need to worry about Y2K. They cut grass with a knife, eat fruit directly from the trees and drink milk from the goats in the backyard."

The nations that would suffer most from an EMP attack would be the modern nations that rely on electricity and computers. Because America depends on sophisticated electronic equipment, this form of attack could result in more long-term damage and death than a nuclear attack on a major city. Only taking major precautions now by hardening our new sewage systems and power grids could help lessen such an attack.

Could something of this magnitude create the effects that John penned in the Book of Revelation, saying that peace would be taken from the earth and people would kill one another with a great sword?

In the northern Golan Heights of Israel, there are numerous large and rugged mountains. The same is true on the east bank of the Jordan River. According to the prophet Ezekiel, the main region of fighting during the war of God and Magog will be in Bashan, the upper Golan Heights in the mountainous region of northern Israel; and in a valley located in the high mountains of Jordan east of the Dead Sea.

In such nations as Iran, Afghanistan and Pakistan, the mountains are so rugged and steep that jeeps, tanks and mobile land vehicles are almost impossible to use. Horses, however, can be used and have been used in recent battles. The Soviet army in Afghanistan was defeated by Afghan fighters riding on horses!

Many tribes in the Middle East and southern Russia use horses to travel across the mountains. It is not impossible to imagine how horses would be used in this future battle. It is also interesting to note that many of the Islamic countries surrounding Israel are the nations that use horses in their daily lives.

Beheading of People

One prophecy in the Book of Revelation has been criticized by liberal scholars for centuries. In fact, these doubt-peddlers relegate the Book of Revelation to some mysterious and strange book whose message applied only to the first century. The prophecy says:

> And I saw thrones, and they sat on them, and judgment was committed to them. Then I saw the souls of those who had been beheaded for their witness to Jesus and for the word of God, who had not worshiped the beast or his image, and had not received his mark on their foreheads or on their hands. And they lived and reigned with Christ for a thousand years (Revelation 20:4).

This scripture indicates that during the final seven-year Tribulation, people who turn their faith toward Jesus Christ will face execution by beheading. In the Greek text, the phrase "I saw souls beheaded" literally reads *I saw souls who were beheaded with the ax.* Modern commentators point out that nations today no longer behead people; men are slain by guns and bombs, not by a sword.

Since the beginning of the War on Terror, the entire world has been shocked to see a group of masked Islamic fanatics reading a decree against an innocent man or woman and then literally cutting his head off. The teachings of Mohammad in the Qur'an indicate that beheading is permitted:

> I will cast terror into the hearts of those who disbelieve. Therefore strike off their heads and strike off every fingertip of them. This is because they acted adversely to Allah and His Apostle (8:12, 13).
>
> Seize them and kill them wherever you find them (4:89).
>
> When you meet the unbelievers in the battlefield strike off their heads and, when you have laid them low, bind your captives firmly (47:4)

When a few United States troops were photographed humiliating men in a prison in Iraq, practically every Islamic leader in the region went into a rage as Arab newspapers and journalists united to condemn and demand the punishment of soldiers who would humiliate these possible terrorists. The same Islamic world was strangely silent, however, when pictures of violent fanatics beheading western businessmen in Iraq hit the internet.

Why were these same leaders who pretended to be violently upset at the Abu Ghraib prison incident nonchalant about a human body without a head on it? Because Islam not only believes in beheading, several of the large Muslim nations also practice it!

Many years ago my father pastored a man who worked for the C.I.A. This man spoke seven languages and was a high ranking agent for the government. On one occasion he was in Saudi Arabia and witnessed a series of beheadings. He said it was not done by a sword, however; the victims were buried in the sand with only their heads sticking out. A giant vehicle with a sharp blade then moved over the bodies, severing the heads from the shoulders.

When we read John's description that many souls would be beheaded, we realize that the only religion in the world whose holy books and religious faith endorses and practices the act of beheading is the religion of Islam. This is one of many reasons I believe the final world dictator identified in the Bible as the Antichrist, will actually be a Muslim (see my book *Unleashing the Beast*).

Weapons in the Wrong Hands

I, along with many others, believe it is only a matter of time until chemical, biological, radiological and nuclear weapons will be in the wrong hands. Civilized, democratic nations will not use their weapons stockpiles to randomly kill innocent people or to perform ethnic cleansing.

When a dictator imparts his ideas to the minds of his followers, however, people will often follow the instructions of their leader blindly, and set out to kill as many of the enemies of their cause as they can find.

Weapons in the hands of such people will cause widespread fear and panic. Jesus foresaw this day and spoke of "men's hearts failing them from fear and the expectation of those things which are coming on the earth" (Luke 21:26).

The Islamic Link

Muslims around the world await the appearance of the Mahdi. While the Qur'an does not make mention of this person, the Hadith, an Islamic holy book alleged to be the sayings of Mohammad overheard by his followers, has about 50 hadiths related to the coming Mahdi. The Bible predicts a coming prince who will make a special covenant with many for a period of seven years (Daniel 9:27). This period is known to scholars and early church fathers as the Tribulation, a seven-year period when the Antichrist will rise.

In Islamic tradition, the coming Mahdi is believed to rule for seven years:

> Abu Saiis al-Khudri said that the Messenger of Allah . . . said, "The Mahdi will be of my stock and will have a broad forehead and a hooked nose. He will fill the earth with equity and justice as it was previously filled with oppression and tyranny, and he will rule for seven years."

> According to Abu Hurayra, the Prophet (Mohammad) . . . said, "The Mahdi will remain in my community for at least seven, or perhaps eight or nine years."

In both the Qur'an and the Hadith, Jesus is called Isa ibn Maryam (Jesus, the son of Mary). Muslims believe Jesus was a prophet but not the Son of God; they firmly deny that Allah has a son. Muslims believe, however, that Jesus will return to Jerusalem, and deny the Trinity and kill all Jews and Christians who oppose Him and the Mahdi:

> Ibn al-Jawziyya says in Ighatha al-Lahfan, "The Muslims are waiting for the descent of the Messiah Isa ibn Maryam from heaven, when he will break the crosses, kill the pigs (Jews) and kill his enemies among the Jews and Christians who worship him. They are

> waiting for the Mahdi to emerge from the House of the Prophets and fill the earth with justice as it is now filled with injustice."

Muslims believe that both the Mahdi and Jesus will appear in Jerusalem, and that they will defeat the Jews and Christians, and actually kill those who do not receive the Mahdi. The standard method of execution in Islam is by the sword, or by beheading.

> Strike off the heads of the infidels wherever you find them.

According to the Book of Revelation, many people will be beheaded during the seven-year Tribulation, because they will refuse to worship the beast or his image:

> *And I saw thrones, and they sat upon them, and judgment was given unto them: and I saw the souls of them that were beheaded for the witness of Jesus, and for the word of God, and which had not worshipped the beast, neither his image, neither had received his mark upon their foreheads, or in their hands; and they lived and reigned with Christ a thousand years* (Revelation 20:4).

The White Horse—the Mahdi?

Some Muslims actually study the prophetic scriptures of the Bible and attempt to use certain prophecies to demonstrate how Islam will fulfill certain predictions in the Qur'an and the Hadith. A vivid illustration of this is in the book published by Muslims, *Al Mahdi* by Muhammad ibn 'Izzat and Muhammad 'Arif. The authors quote the Book of Revelation, concerning the rider on a white horse:

> *And I saw, and behold a white horse: and he that sat on him had a bow; and a crown was given unto*

him: and he went forth conquering, and to conquer (Revelation 6:2).

They comment:

> It is clear that this man is the Mahdi who will ride a white horse and judge by the Qur'an (with justice) and with whom will be men with the marks of prostration on their foreheads (Muhammad ibn 'Izzat and Muhammad 'Arif, Al Mahdi and the End of Time. (London: Dar Al Taqwa Ltd., 1997) 15.

These two Muslim writers then adopt the symbolism of the woman clothed with the sun, who has the moon under her feet and the 12 stars on her head, and who brings forth the man-child to rule the nations. They write:

> The description of this extraordinary woman clearly indicates Fatima as-Zahra from whose descendants will come from Mahdi (p. 15).

The Ark of the Covenant and the Mahdi

Rumors of finding the location of the Ark of the Covenant have intrigued people for years. The Ark of the Covenant was a gold chest built by Moses in the wilderness that once contained the tablets of the Law, the rod of Aaron and a golden pot of manna (Hebrew 9:4).

The Ark was the most sacred piece of furniture in the Tabernacle of Moses and in the Temple of Solomon. It was believed to have been hidden before the Babylonian captivity, and its special hiding place was never found. Several Jewish organizations in Jerusalem, including the director of the Temple Institute, believe the Ark is hidden in a secret chamber under the Temple Mount.

This theory was confirmed to me when I interviewed Rabbi Yehuda Getz, a former rabbi in Israel, who claimed to have seen the ark in the early 1980s. When asked why the Ark was not removed from its hiding place, he said it was in a damaged condition and the Jews have no purification ritual with which to purify the Levites to carry the sacred box. Besides, there is no Temple in which to place it and no priesthood in authority to minister.

It is, according to Getz, actually safer in its location than it would be in public. He said it would cause a war with the Muslims because Jews would be determined to build another Temple on the Temple Mount if the Ark was recovered.

In the year 2000, I conducted a Partner's Tour of Israel and taped a Manna-Fest program in front of the famous Eastern Gate in Jerusalem. I shared some of the information about the possible location of the Ark of the Covenant being hidden under the Temple Mount. After the program aired I received a phone call from a retired United States colonel. He was quite upset, and said he had been told by the Justice Department to contact me and ask me not to air the program again. He received information that several Muslim nations had made copies of two of our programs which had some rather "sensitive information."

A short time after the information was viewed on television and satellite, Yassir Arafat began a series of expansion programs under the Temple Mount itself, in an underground area known as Solomon's Stables. Tons of debris was removed from the site, which included portions of columns from Herod's Temple.

A special door was made, giving worshippers access to the underground chambers. This was designed to become another large mosque. Thus, the Temple Mount area now has three

Muslim mosques: the Dome of the Rock, the al-Aqsa and the new underground chamber.

A rumor spread that the Muslims may have been trying to find the Ark of the Covenant. Strangely, some religious Jews, Christians and Muslims believe the Ark may be recovered in the future. As-Suyuti wrote, "At the hands of the Mahdi the Ark of the Covenant will be brought forth at Lake Tiberias and placed in Jerusalem." Another Muslim writer, Sulayman ibn 'Isa, said, "When the Jews see it (the Ark) they will become Muslims except for a few of them."

We know from Bible prophecy that some form of a Jewish Temple on the Temple Mount will exist during the first 42 months of the Tribulation. I am of the opinion that Elijah the Prophet, one of the two witnesses of Revelation 11:1-3, will help "restore all things." This includes a new Temple and bringing the religious Jews the knowledge of which tribe they are from. This was taught by the early fathers of the Christian faith.

After 42 months, the Antichrist will invade Jerusalem, killing the two witnesses and liberating half of Jerusalem from all Jewish and Christian presence. It is possible that the discovery of the Ark will trigger the rebuilding of a Temple, enraging the Muslim population. The supernatural power of the two witnesses to bring death to their enemies will cause such fear that no Muslim or Jew will be willing to attack the two prophets (Revelation 11:3-6).

These are just a few of the major predictions being written and circulated throughout the Islamic world. They are preached in the mosques and taught in the madrassas. The knowledge of these things gives a person better insight into why Muslims are interested in the last days, and why defeating the west and bringing the Mahdi into power is on their minds.

Do not be afraid of sudden terror, nor of trouble from the wicked when it comes; for the Lord will be your confidence (Proverbs 3:25, 26).

5

The Next Strike on American Soil

A strange lull has settled over America since 9/11. Special agents from government organizations have pulled financial and intelligent resources together, and a large dent has been made in the possible plans of terrorists. The lack of visible activity seems to be lulling Americans to sleep, however.

We must remember that the gap of time between the first attack on the World Trade Center in 1993 and the September 11, 2001 assault was a period of nearly nine years. The individuals who join "sleeper cells" have extreme patience and will wait for years before initiating another big attack.

I have spoken personally with both Israeli and American military personnel directly involved in counter-terrorism, and they all say it is only a matter of time before we experience another strike on American soil.

Various opinions are heard about what a terror group could actually do. Counter-terror organizations who intercept internet "chatter," indicate the plans for the next attack will be much more dramatic and cost more lives than 9/11. In an interview on Al-Jazeera, the mideast television channel, Osama bin Laden admitted in 2001 that he was actively trying to collect more chemical, biological and nuclear weapons. Some suggest that a dirty bomb will be used. According to insiders, several dirty bomb components were confiscated in a shipping terminal in the Chicago area. An arrest was then made, and the accused was allegedly plotting to construct a dirty bomb.

In 1998, Sultan Bashiruddin Mahmood, western-educated nuclear physicist and former chairman of the Pakistan Atomic Energy Commission, was hailed by Pakistanis as a hero for his work in developing Pakistan's first nuclear bomb. He left that job to become the head of Pakistan's secret service. Later, he was dismissed from his government job because he had become an Islamic fanatic with close ties to the Taliban in Afghanistan. After his arrest he told of discussing radiological material and dirty bombs with bin Laden in Kabul in August, 2001.

One month after the September 11 attacks, the U.S. Army and CIA intelligence intercepted communications between Mahmood and the Taliban leader, Mullah Omar. Eventually, the Mahmood's residence was searched, and in the building were drawings of a helium hot-air balloon designed to release large quantities of anthrax spores. What was even more frightening was that according to Mahmood, he was in contact with Osama bin Laden in August of 2001, and the terrorist mastermind had revealed that he possessed radioactive material and was interested in making a "dirty nuke." Bin Laden asked him how the material he had could be made into a weapon or something usable.

The Black Wind of Death

I believe it is possible that the second wave against the United States will come in the form of a chemical or a biological attack. I base this on intelligence information and on a statement made by an al-Qaeda leader that an Islamic prophecy predicted would occur at "the end of days."

On March 11, 2003, the newspaper *Al-Quds al-Arabi* received a five-page e-mail from the Brigade of Abu Hafs al-Masri, claiming its "death squad" had penetrated Spain. This e-mail contained an ominous warning for America:

> We announce the good news for Muslims in the world that the strike of the black wind of death, the expected strike against America, is now at its final stage—90 percent ready—and is coming soon, by God's will.

I recall journalists and commentators discussing the meaning of the phrase, "black wind of death." Some have suggested it is hidden code or a cryptic term for the name of a future attack. Others believe it suggests a chemical or biological attack. Actually, "smoke" is mentioned in Islamic predictions as a sign of the last days. In 44:10, 11, the Qur'an says:

> Then watch thou for the Day that the sky will bring forth a kind of smoke (or mist) plainly visible, enveloping the people. This will be the grievous chastisement.

An Islamic commentary elaborates on this saying:

> *The appearance of smoke is one of the major portents of the Last Hour. This noxious cloud of smoke will spread all over the world. True believers*

may feel from this smoke the sensation of a common
cold or catarrh, while it will reach at each and every
nook and corner of the unbelievers and hypocrites;
resulting in their demise by suffocation and asphyxia.

In Islamic tradition, the four winds are similar to the four horsemen of the Apocalypse in Revelation 6. The black wind may depict an intentional economic disaster as a direct result of a terrorist attack. The black wind may be associated with black dust; or it may depict the outbreak of a virus carried by an agent that disperses it. Many viruses, like smallpox, are capable of being misused this way.

Islamic writers have a variety of opinions as to what this "smoke" actually alludes to. Some take it as a supernatural sign sent by Allah against the unbelievers. Others indicate it will be something Muslims will initiate; however, they will be protected from this chastisement by Allah.

This portent is one of the many signs that, according to Islamic teachers, will precede the arrival of the Mahdi. As one Islamic writer pointed out: "A black wind (will) arise, and there will be earthquakes in which many will be killed."

I believe this prediction could actually become self-fulfilling. That is, a group of Islamic fanatics will develop a chemical or biological agent that will manifest itself as a visible form of smoke. It could come from a type of bomb that will cause death to those with whom it comes in contact.

Apocalyptic Muslims are as certain that their predictions will come to pass as religious Jews believe in a coming Messiah and Christians believe in the Biblical signs of Christ's return. By initiating such an attack, they will signal to all Muslims that the last days are here and their long-awaited leader will bring the world under Islamic dominion.

100,000 in the Next Attack

A person named Abu Salma al-Hijazi, the al Qaeda commander in Iraq and a close associate of bin Laden, was interviewed in Iraq months after the liberation by the United States and coalition forces. The Middle East Media Research Institute (MEMRI) asked this al Qaeda "commander" about a large-scale future strike against the United States of America.

Al-Hijazi was quoted as saying, "A huge and very courageous strike will take place and the number of infidels expected to be killed in this attack, according to primary estimates, exceeds 100,000." He added that he anticipates, but will not swear, that the attack will happen during Ramadan (an Islamic holy month).

He further revealed that when the attack is carried out it would "amaze the world and turn al Qaeda into an organization that horrifies the world until the law of Allah is implemented, and not just in words, on His land. You wait and see that the balance of power between al Qaeda and its rivals will change, all of a sudden, Allah willing."

Attack at a Nuclear Reactor

It is possible a sleeper cell from Canada may have been assigned to bring this prediction to pass. The government in Canada arrested a large sleeper cell known as the "Toronto 19." The original plan of these individuals, it is alleged, was to hijack a plane and then fly it into a nuclear power plant near the border of Canada and America.

America's reactors are built with safety and security in mind. Layers of thick concrete secure the reactors from a plane crash or an earthquake. Terrorists held to the theory that the heat from the burning jet fuel and plane would melt the nuclear fuel rods and produce a deadly cloud of poison. They announced they expected 100,000 Americans to die! This is the number of deaths predicted by Abu Salma al-Hijazi, Osama bin Laden's commander. This "death cloud" could fit into the scenario of the "black wind of death" mentioned in Islamic prophecies.

In evaluating this terrorist's statement, several points can be made. In order for 100,000 people to die at one time, the attack would likely occur in a large city, with the population living close together. It could also occur at a time when people are at work, or it may be linked to a major sports event where thousands are gathered together.

Anthrax in a Sports Stadium

I heard a former member of Saddam's Baath party reveal how Saddam Hussein had made plans to release anthrax during a large sports event. The plan involved a woman with a small child who was nursing, using bottles which held milk. One of the bottles would be a specially made bottle which appeared on the outside to have milk, but had anthrax instead.

During the final period of the game, when the stadium was on its feet, the woman, who would be sitting near one of the tunnels, would open the lid of the bottle and release the anthrax. The swirling wind in the tunnel would circulate the anthrax throughout the stadium. In a few days, thousands would have flu-like symptoms and within a few weeks, thousands would be dead before anyone realized what had occurred.

We know that the drug Cipro can actually help stop the effects of anthrax, *if taken in time.* In a terrorist attack, however, it may be difficult to know who and how many are affected. The anthrax spores may have already damaged those exposed to this deadly agent.

We all recall what one spoonful of anthrax did to the postal service and the Senate building in Washington. A tabloid newspaper building was completely sealed off for months when anthrax was sent to the paper. The tabloid had published a negative article about Osama bin Laden prior to 9/11. It is still a mystery who actually sent the anthrax-laced letters.

Shortly after 9/11, a friend of mine, a California businessman who is originally from Pakistan, told me an interesting story. Thousands of Muslims from various countries of the Middle East live in his area. One afternoon five men, all from different countries of the Middle East, visited his office. During the conversation, the men revealed that they were planning to open a small coffee shop in the area, and wanted to see if he was interested in investing in the business.

The conversation continued, and the men became more comfortable with my friend. A former Muslim, he is now a Christian. The men also invited him to join another possible plan. They implied strongly that he should read between the lines. One man owned crop-dusting planes, and they had a "special plan" for a major event coming to the area.

My friend told them to get back in touch with him later. One of the visitors had a cell phone, and he told my friend to call him and he would meet with him personally. After the men departed, agents with the FBI came to my friend's office and began to question him about his conversation with the five men.

He informed the FBI that he did not know them, but the men claimed to have plans for a coffee shop in the area. He also told them he was very suspicious of something they had said about a "special plan," and was even more suspicious because they were all from different countries.

My friend gave the FBI the cell phone number. Because of the new laws that have been passed, the FBI was able to tap the phone and discover a plot.

A large evangelistic meeting was being planned for a huge stadium, not far from the offices of the businessman. These men were part of a sleeper cell in the area. The man who owned the planes was going to allow a Muslim friend to fly a plane over the stadium during the Christian meeting, and spray gasoline over the crowd. Immediately, a second plane would fly over and crash into the crowd, thus causing a massive fire and the death or severe injury to thousands of believers.

According to my sources, these men were arrested and the plot was stopped. There is no end to what type of attacks could occur, if we are not vigilant and prayerful. Jesus often told us to not be afraid, but to be watchful and prayerful.

In the fall of 2002, the entire Northern Virginia region was in fear as an unknown sniper killed innocent people at gas stations, bus stops and shopping centers. Millions of dollars were spent and millions were lost by restaurants and malls because people were afraid to get out at night.

When the two culprits were discovered, what seemed to slip through the cracks was that the head sniper was a Muslim. The media seemed to downplay this fact, but this was a form of terror attack which was discussed and practiced in the al Qaeda training camps in Afghanistan.

The Pattern of the Next Attack

The Bible tells us: "That which has been is what will be, that which is done is what will be done" (Ecclesiastes 1:9). Often major events that impact the world are previewed in Scripture in the form of a cycle or pattern. Shortly after 9/11, I was ministering in Baton Rouge, Louisiana, at Healing Place Church. During my personal devotional time one day, I was observing a strange pattern in the Book of Job which seemed to be similar to the attack on the World Trade Center.

Job was the wealthiest man in his day, just as the United States is the wealthiest nation on earth. The Book of Job says the attack was sudden and totally unexpected, just as the 9/11 attack was sudden and unexpected. The first assault on Job was a wind that came from heaven and knocked down the "four corners" of the house where Job's children were living. When the "four corners" of the Trade Center collapsed, the dusty grey wind began swirling, layering a blanket of dust over New York.

Job's children died in his tragedy of tragedies. His wealth was impacted as his animals were destroyed by lightning and stolen by the Chaldeans. The attack on the Trade Center impacted not only world trade, but affected the economy of America.

The Chaldeans were a group of nomads from the area of Arabia. The 19 hijackers were predominantly from the same land as the ancient Chaldeans. The grief of Job was so great he could barely speak for seven days. Job spent the week attending the funerals of his children, in the same way New York City's leaders went from funeral to funeral for seven days after 9/11.

In Job's case, there was a lull between the first and second attacks. I recall telling the church that there would be another major attack, but there would be an extended gap of time between the first and the second attacks. The patterns from the story of Job point this out. When the Adversary planned the second attack on Job, he planned a physical attack that produced sores on Job's body and almost cost him his life.

There has been a long gap since the 9/11 attack, but there is no doubt another wave of terror will eventually come to the shores of America. If the first chapter of the Book of Job is a cryptic pattern of the first attack on America, then could the second wave affect the physical bodies of those hit by the attack in the same manner that Job had sores over his body? Only time will tell if these patterns will continue.

Just as Job leaned continuously on God, we as believers must rely continuously on God's protection and grace. We should also have a personal contingency plan for ourselves and for our families.

A prudent man foresees evil and hides himself; the simple pass on and are punished (Proverbs 27:12).

6

Prepared, but Not Scared

In the scripture above, the Hebrew word *prudent* means to be "crafty and subtle." Often we speak of being crafty or subtle in a negative sense, but Jesus said we should "Be wise as serpents and harmless as doves" (Matthew 10:16). A wise man discerns the prophetic times in order to receive the blessings of the season and prepare for the trouble that often arises during major prophetic fulfillment.

Some people consider prophetic end-time preaching too negative, and therefore refuse to listen to any teacher or speaker who deals with the time of the end. Thankfully, this was not the attitude of Noah when he was warned of the coming flood. The Bible says:

> *By faith Noah, being divinely warned of things not yet seen, moved with godly fear, prepared an ark*

for the saving of his household, by which he condemned the world and became heir of the righteousness which is according to faith (Hebrews 11:7).

Noah had a good dose of the fear of the Lord. He knew if he did not prepare, his family would be destroyed in the coming flood that God had promised. Noah responded over 100 years before the flood arrived by preparing the ark to save his household (Genesis 6:3).

I often say that prophetic preaching is not to scare you but to prepare you. Dealing with the possibilities of future chemical, biological and nuclear attacks is certainly a fearful thought. Jesus said men's hearts would fail them for fear, and for looking after those things that are coming on the earth (Luke 21:26).

Yet, the believer knows how to prepare for and ride out the storm in the same way Noah used the ark to ride out the flood and save his household.

+ If the local news told you a severe storm was coming with 25 inches of rain and your area was going to flood, would you sit at home and watch videos all night while the water was rising at your front door?
+ If the weather service said a tornado was spotted in your vicinity, would you stand at the window and wait for its arrival, or take shelter in the basement?
+ If an armed criminal escaped from prison and was in your neighborhood, would you let your children out to play?

In the same manner, we know that another attack will come. We do not know when, where or how it will come; but a prudent person will prepare, not in fear, but because a prepared person is less likely to panic under severe circumstances.

The Threat Analysis

According to Homeland Security the most severe terror threats against America can be placed in four categories:

- The Biological Threat
- The Chemical Threat
- The Nuclear Threat
- The Dirty Bomb Threat

The Biological Threat. A biological attack would include various types of germs that, when released, would cause a person to get sick. A biological attack would more than likely involve something that would be inhaled, or perhaps enter the skin through a cut. Some viruses, such as smallpox, can be caught from other people.

If someone receives an unknown substance in the mail, or sees or smells a strange substance in the air, he should report it to the authorities as soon as possible. It is best to get away from the area and cover your mouth with layers of fabric or cloth.

The Chemical Threat. A chemical attack can come in the form of a liquid, a gas or a solid. Some possible signs of exposure to a chemical are extreme watering of the eyes, twitching, coughing or losing one's breath. An extreme attack can cause loss of coordination. One sign of possible chemical release are dead animals, such as birds. If such signs occur, take precautions and get away from the area as quickly as possible.

If the attack is in a building, a person should try to exit the facility without coming through the contaminated area. If a person is on the outside, they must choose to leave the area in the opposite direction of the chemical release or enter a safe "sealed room."

If your eyes water, your skin begins to sting and you begin having trouble breathing, you may have been exposed to a chemical. You should immediately strip and wash, using a hose, a fountain or any source of water. Do not scrub the chemical into your skin. Medical attention should be sought immediately.

The Nuclear Threat. The greatest danger in a nuclear attack is the radioactive contamination that follows the blast. The trademark sign of a nuclear attack is the huge fireball and pillar of smoke that follows. Radioactive fallout is the dust, or particulate matter, produced by a nuclear explosion and carried high up into the air by the mushroom cloud. It drifts on the wind and most of it settles back to earth downwind of the explosion.

The heaviest, most dangerous and most noticeable fallout, occurs close to ground zero. It may begin arriving minutes after an explosion, but the smaller and lighter dust-like particles will typically be arriving hours later, as they drift much farther downwind. Fallout often occurs for hundreds of miles. As the fallout settles, whether you see it or not, it will accumulate and blow around everywhere, just like dust or light snow. Wind and rain concentrate the fallout into localized "hot spots" of much more intense radiation with no visible indication of its presence.

This radioactive "dust" is dangerous because it emits penetrating radiation energy similar to x-rays. The radiation (not the fallout dust) can go through walls, roofs and protective clothing. Even if you manage not to inhale or ingest the dust, keep it off your skin, hair and clothes. Even if none gets inside your house, the radiation penetrating your home is still extremely dangerous and can injure or kill you inside.

Radioactive fallout from a nuclear explosion, though very dangerous initially, loses its intensity quickly because it is giving off so much energy. Scientists tell us that fallout loses

90 percent of its deadly energy within seven hours of the initial explosion, and 99 percent in two days. That is really good news, because our families can readily survive it *if* we get them into a proper shelter to safely wait it out as it becomes less dangerous with every passing hour.

The Dirty Bomb Threat. A dirty bomb uses a conventional explosion mixed with radioactive material. If you should find yourself in an area where a dirty bomb attack occurs, you can expect localized and downwind contamination from the explosion and dispersed radioactive materials. If you are near enough to see or hear the bomb blast, assume that it includes radiological or chemical agents.

The danger of this type of explosion is that you may not know right away that the bomb contained radioactive materials. So move away from the blast area as quickly as possible. If the wind is blowing toward you from the direction of the blast, travel in a direction that keeps the wind to your left or right as you move away from the blast area. If possible cover your face with a dust mask or cloth to avoid inhaling potentially radioactive dust.

When you reach a safe location, remove your outer clothing while you are still outside, and shower as soon as possible. Refer to local news sources for additional instructions about shelter or evacuation. The government is better prepared to direct and assist the public in a "dirty bomb" incident than it is an actual nuclear weapon attack.

Emergency Supplies

Persons living in areas frequented by hurricanes, tornados and flooding are aware of the necessity of emergency preparedness. Every home should have certain items set aside, in the event of a power blackout or an extended storm.

Water. Store enough supplies for a gallon of water a day for each day. We have in our basement several boxes of bottled water that can be rotated every few months.

Food. It is good to have a supply of nonperishable food that will not go bad, and can be eaten without being heated or cooked. These items can include protein and fruit bars, dry cereal, canned food and juices. Remember that a major attack could stop trucks from delivering food items for an extended period of time. Don't forget any plates, spoons, forks, cups and other items that may be needed, including sanitary supplies.

Clean Air

Staying at Home. Hopefully, most people would be able to stay at home under most circumstances if certain types of attacks occurred in their area. Several years ago, the media mocked Tom Ridge, America's first secretary of Homeland Security, when he suggested that Americans purchase duct tape and plastic to cover windows and doors in the event of a major chemical or biological attack. Often an explosion will release fine particles of unknown material into the air.

Most people who work at a store or own a store will not be hanging around doing business in an emergency; they will be on the move with friends and families. Banks, gas stations and food stores will be closed. If the population in a major city is asked to move, many cars will run out of gas before arriving at their destination. Cash and gas are important items when suddenly departing an area. If hundreds or thousands of vehicles are on the road, everyone will be seeking gasoline, food and water.

Emergency Travel Pack. Always keep an emergency travel pack ready. The items marked with an asterisk should be in your emergency pack. The emergency pack should include:

- A small supply of cash
- Any food needed for the road or a brief stay
- Any water needed
- Any medicine needed
- Any change of clothes or diapers needed

Emergency Travel. Should you find it necessary to leave your home in a hurry, you should be prepared.

- Know the roads and routes going in and out of your city.
- Be sure you have enough gasoline for more than a few miles.
- Be sure you have an ample supply of cash if needed.
- Know where you can stay in any direction in which you may need to travel.

Disaster Supplies Kit

The Red Cross and Federal Emergency Management Agency (FEMA) recommends certain items for a Disaster Supplies Kit. They suggest stocking six basics for your home: water, food, first aid supplies, clothing and bedding, tools and emergency supplies, and special items. Keep the items you would most likely need in an easy-to-carry container, should you have to leave home in a hurry. Possible containers include a large covered trash container, a camping backpack or a duffle bag.

Water. Store water in plastic containers. Avoid using containers that will decompose or break, such as milk cartons or glass bottles. A normally active person needs to drink at least two quarts of water each day. Hot environments and intense physical activity can double that amount. Children, nursing mothers and people who are ill need more.

- Store a gallon of water per person per day. Keep at least two quarts for drinking and two quarts for food preparation and sanitation needs.
- For safety reasons, replenish your water supply every six months.

Food

- Store at least a three-day supply of nonperishable food.
- Select foods that require no refrigeration, preparation or cooking; and little or no water.
- If you have food you must heat, pack a can of sterno.
- Select food items that are compact and lightweight.
- *Include a selection of the following foods:*
  - Ready-to-eat canned meats, fruits and vegetables
  - Canned juices
  - Staples (salt, sugar, pepper, spices, etc.)
  - High-energy foods
  - Vitamins
  - Food for infants
  - Comfort/stress foods

First Aid Kit*

Assemble a first aid kit for your home and one for each car the family drives. Include:

- 20 adhesive bandages (various sizes)
- 5" x 9" sterile dressing
- Conforming roller gauze bandage
- Triangular bandages

- 3 x 3 sterile gauze pads
- 4 x 4 sterile gauze pads
- One roll of 3" cohesive bandage
- Two germicidal hand wipes or waterless, alcohol-based hand sanitizer
- Six antiseptic wipes
- Two pairs of large medical-grade, non-latex gloves
- Adhesive tape 2" width
- Anti-bacterial ointment
- Cold pack
- Scissors (small, personal) and tweezers
- CPR breathing barrier, such as a face shield.

Non-Prescription Drugs*

- Aspirin or non-aspirin pain reliever
- Anti-diarrhea medication
- Antacid (for stomach upset), and laxative
- Syrup of Ipecac (to induce vomiting)
- Activated charcoal (use only on advice of the Poison Control Center)

Tools and Supplies

- Mess kits, or paper cups, plates and plastic utensils
- Emergency preparedness manual
- Battery-operated radio and extra batteries
- Flashlight and extra batteries
- Cash or traveler's checks, change
- Non-electric can opener, utility knife
- Fire extinguisher: small canister ABC type
- Tube tent

- Pliers
- Tape
- Matches in a waterproof container
- Aluminum foil
- Plastic storage containers
- Signal flare, compass
- Paper and pencils
- Needles and thread
- Medicine dropper
- Shut-off wrench to turn off the household gas and water
- Whistle
- Plastic sheeting
- Map of the area (for locating shelters)

Sanitation

- Toilet paper, towelettes*
- Soap, liquid detergent*
- Feminine supplies*
- Personal hygiene items*
- Plastic garbage bags and ties for personal sanitation use*
- Plastic bucket with tight lid
- Disinfectant*
- Household chlorine bleach

Clothing and Bedding

- Include at least one complete change of clothing and footwear per person.*

- Sturdy shoes or work boots
- Rain gear*
- Blankets or sleeping bags*
- Hat and gloves
- Thermal underwear
- Sunglasses

Special Items

Remember those family members with special requirements. Remember especially the needs of infants and the elderly or disabled persons

For Baby*

- Formula
- Diapers
- Bottles
- Powdered milk
- Medications

For Adults*

- Heart and high blood pressure medication
- Insulin
- Prescription drugs
- Denture needs
- Contact lenses and supplies
- Extra eye glasses

Inspiration and Entertainment

- Study Bible
- Games and books
- Other personal inspirational material

Important Family Documents

Keep these records in a waterproof, portable container:

- Will, insurance policies, contracts, deeds, stocks and bonds
- Passports, social security cards, immunization records
- Bank account numbers
- Credit card account numbers and companies
- Inventory of valuable household goods, important telephone numbers
- Family records (birth, marriage, death certificates)

Store your kit in a convenient place known to all family members. Keep a smaller version of the supplies kit in the trunk of your car. Keep all items in airtight plastic bags.

Change your stored water supply every six months so that it stays fresh. Replace your stored food every six months. Rethink your kit and family needs at least once a year. Replace batteries, update clothes, etc.

Consult your physician or pharmacist about storing prescription medications.

As we approach the end of this age and the coming of Jesus Christ, more and more we will see the disastrous signs of earth's birth pains as it anticipates God's final triumph (see Romans 8:22). We will also see, more and more, the terror and evil of wicked men and this world's ungodly, satanic system.

As overcoming believers, we refuse to live our lives in fear. We already know the end of history! So we live our days in a state of readiness, "looking for the blessed hope and glorious appearing of our great God and Savior Jesus Christ" (Titus 2:13).

Nations are in an uproar, kingdoms fall; he lifts his voice, the earth melts. The Lord Almighty is with us, the God of Jacob is our fortress (Psalm 46:6, 7, NIV).

7

Important Summary

I have traveled to the Middle East over 26 times and have had the opportunity to personally meet Jews, Palestinian Christians and Muslims. I have discovered that just as all Christians are not alike—some are dedicated and others are Christian in name only—the same holds true for people in the Islamic religion. My personal observation is that individuals who claim Islam as their religion can be divided into three camps.

1. Secular (non-committed Muslims)
2. Moderate (committed Muslims)
3. Fundamentalist (radical Muslims)

Secular Muslims can be found in scattered pockets throughout the Middle East, Europe and in America. They have blended in with western ideas and concepts, and attend the mosque out of respect for their relatives and family. I've met some personally who never pray the five required prayers a day, never make the Hajj to Mecca, and keep the Islamic teachings that benefit them in the community. This small group listens to other opinions, and are often the quickest to receive the gospel.

Moderate Muslims make up the larger percentage of Muslims throughout the world. These are Muslims who attend the mosque, follow the regulations of dress and personal conduct in the Qur'an and the Hadith, and work an honest job to provide for their families. These Muslims are the general population in Turkey, Jordan, parts of Indonesia and other moderate Islamic nations.

Fundamentalist Muslims are those who are inclined to take the word of Mohammad to conduct a holy war (jihad) against Christians and Jews as a literal command for this day and time. These are the ones who preach hatred for the people of the Book (Jews and Christians), and encourage suicide bombings, terrorism against the west and death to Jews and Israel. Some suggest that as many as 200 million Muslims may fit this category.

In breaking down these three categories, I suggest that we be careful not to classify all Muslims as fanatical or possible terrorists. While all practicing Muslims believe in the signs of the last days, there are pockets of Muslims who have no desire to slay an "infidel" and do not accept the terrorist ideology of using terrorism as a tool for jihad. The possible 200 million fundamentalists scattered throughout the globe, however, are the ones who create concern.

This group appears to be organizing, with the idea of helping to initiate the last days by fulfilling the Islamic prophecies concerning the arrival of al Mahdi. Just as Christians believe they should preach the gospel around the world and then the end will come (Matthew 24:14), so Apocalyptic Muslims believe their role in bringing about the conversion of the world to Islam is the defeat of the west and Israel. As I have pointed out, the only way to defeat the western powers, in the eyes of the fanatics, is by terrorizing their cities.

Once a person understands the unusual Islamic prediction for the last days, and compares the present prophetic activity in Israel, Iraq, Afghanistan, London and America, then the reason for terrorism becomes clear. They see terrorism with bombs and with chemical, biological and nuclear weapons are tools of Allah in the hands of Jihad warriors to bring down the infidel governments and exalt a new world order of Islamic expectations.

Using Our Freedoms Against Us

It may seem ludicrous to suggest that America's freedoms could eventually destroy her from within, but this is the opinion of one of Israel's great political leaders. I heard him state that the enemies of America living among us are using our freedom against us. Our own freedoms can, at times, prevent our intelligence agencies from investigating individuals who might be future terrorists or enemies of the nation.

During the early 1970s, my father pastored a church in Northern Virginia. Several people in his church held high-level jobs in the federal government, including the area of intelligence services. One man, a high-level CIA agent, told my father that the greatest danger to America was Islamic fanatics and terrorists who were entering the country.

He stated that "the agency" had warned three American presidents that many of the young men entering the country from Islamic countries on student visas, were actually linked, at that time, to the Palestine Liberation Organization (PLO). He said they had links to Yassir Arafat, and could easily become active terrorists on American soil.

According to this man, the three presidents who were warned blew off the warnings. Their argument was, "As a free and open nation, we cannot stop these individuals from coming to our country to be educated and to experience the freedoms we enjoy." The same thing could be said of the 19 hijackers who on 9/11 turned peaceful commuter jaunts into flights of death. Those 19 extremists had the "right" to come to America and the "right" to be trained in our own flight schools, but they turned our know-how into weapons against our own people.

A great concern of mine today is the manufactured anguish of the left wing over how we treat the terrorists at Guantanamo Bay. Politicians have complained that the air conditioners didn't even work, and the place is too hot for those men! They choose to ignore—or they are too ignorant to realize—the fact that these terrorists come from the mountains of Pakistan and Afghanistan where the tents they live in are not air conditioned.

The same brain-dead voices of American liberalism complain when a Qur'an is mishandled by a guard, but silently accept the fact that Christians in America cannot pray or read the Bible openly. The same silly elected officials defend the ACLU for removing every trace of Christianity they can from the face of America.

In the name of freedom we keep our borders open on both Canada and Mexico. When a group of patriotic men agreed to stand guard at the border of Arizona and Mexico to stop illegal immigrants, the results spoke for themselves. Word was out in Mexico, *Avoid that area*! However, the talking heads of freedom's liberal television networks demanded these "evil persons" be removed, and prevented from keeping the illegal interlopers from pouring into the country.

The liberal press in Great Britain must have attended the same universities as some of our incompetent officials. They too were against any regulations in controlling, profiling or stopping hate speeches among Muslim groups in Britain—that is, until the torn bodies of 58 innocent victims were pulled from the twisted metal of a bus and the subway. Suddenly, the outspoken critics had nothing to say.

It reminded me of the reaction of the ACLU. This anti-Christian organization thrives on lawsuits against the Bible, against Christians or against anything that carries the name of God. They support and defend some of the most perverted people caught doing the most perverted things. When 9/11 came and millions of Americans throughout the land were seen praying, the ACLU went into the closet for a brief time. They filed no lawsuits in the month of September. In that season American patriots would have tarred and feathered any lawyer foolish enough to sue New Yorkers for praying in public.

I suspect the same will be true in the future. When terrorists cross our borders with weapons of mass destruction and once again strike at America's heart and soul, slaying thousands of innocent people, the liberals will suddenly "see the light" and talk about the need to profile a few people, check out a few mosques and protect our borders.

But for those who suffer in the next wave of terrorism, all the talk and rhetoric will be too late. We are in a new war and will be, in one form or another, until the return of Christ. Our best defense is prayer and the protection of the Almighty. We must increase our understanding and knowledge to know what we are dealing with—and why. Our greatest weapon is the gospel of Jesus Christ. It can change the hard hearts of men and cause them to love those they seek to destroy.

In many Islamic nations, the loving truth that Jesus Christ died for you, and you can go to heaven by receiving Him, is striking a responsive chord among the next generation of Muslims. The only way a Palestinian can love a Jew, a Jew love a Christian and a Christian love a Muslim is when they believe and receive the gospel. Then we are no longer Jew, Muslim or Christian, we are simply believers and brothers.

Closing Remarks

A person may never understand why Muslims in Iraq are killing other Muslims (or why American forces are being resisted when, in reality, they have liberated 25 million souls from a tyrant) unless he understands some of the Islamic prophecies linking Iraq to the appearing of Islam's final leader.

American troops in Iraq create a unique situation for Muslims. If the west influences the government of Iraq, then this could diminish the belief among Muslims of the coming al Mahdi. Peace and prosperity in Iraq would diminish the influence of the Mahdi teaching and there would be no need for the tradition to continue. This is one of the fears of neighboring nations, such as Iran.

The longer foreign troops are present, the longer it will be before the "enlightened one" can appear. After all, the foreign "occupation" gives authority to the occupier. All of this creates real consternation and frustration among Muslims who have studied their prophecies and have anticipated the arrival of their own messiah.

Average Americans cannot figure it all out, and will not be able to do so unless they have a basic understanding of how Muslims view the future and how their predictions must shortly come to pass. I believe this book has given you a general understanding and will help you to better see why the conflict continues, and the war of terrorism is only beginning.

The good news is that these events are also signs to the Christian that Jesus Christ is soon returning! Don't lose faith and don't let your heart be troubled. He who promised to prepare a place for us also promised to return again (John 14:1, 2). These events are signs to identify the times in which we live. Yes, it can be frightening; but, at the same time, exciting to know that the Lord will return to set up His Millenial Kingdom!

> Then I saw an angel coming down from heaven, having the key to the bottomless pit and a great chain in his hand. He laid hold of the dragon, that serpent of old, who is the Devil and Satan, and bound him for a thousand years; and he cast him into the bottomless pit, and shut him up, and set a seal on him, so that he should deceive the nations no more till the thousand years were finished. But after these things he must be released for a little while.
>
> And I saw thrones, and they sat on them, and judgment was committed to them. Then I saw the souls of those who had been beheaded for their witness to Jesus and for the word of God, who had not worshiped the beast or his image, and had not received his mark on their foreheads or on their hands. And they lived and reigned with Christ for a thousand years (Revelation 20:1-4).

How To Be Saved

STEP 1: REALIZE THAT YOU ARE A SINNER AND FOR YOUR SOUL TO BE SAVED, YOU NEED TO COME TO GOD.

God created us to have a relationship with Him. He wants us to experience true and lasting peace in this life. Blaise Pascal, the French philosopher and mathematician, said, "There is a God-shaped vacuum in the heart of every man which cannot be filled by any created thing, but only by God, the Creator, made known through Jesus."

The Bible confirms what we already know: "All have sinned and fall short of the glory of God" (Romans 3:23). This is the reason the peace of God eludes you in your vain search for reality: "Your iniquities have separated you from your God; and your sins have hidden His face from you" (Isaiah 59:2). Reality is knowing Him!

STEP 2: ACKNOWLEDGE THE FACT THAT YOU CANNOT SAVE YOURSELF.

There is a way that seems right to a man, but its end is the way of death (Proverbs 14:12).

Nothing you try works. Regardless of which path you choose, it seems, the peace of God eludes you. Your own attempts to solve your problems have ended in disaster.

You have tried good works and found your efforts to be meaningless, empty, without Christ. Riches cannot buy salvation. Fame or good breeding does not impress God. Personal suffering cannot save. Yet, you realize you desperately need the touch of God in your life!

STEP 3: BELIEVE THAT JESUS CHRIST CAN AND WILL SAVE YOU!

Jesus said . . , "I am the way, the truth, and the life. No one comes to the Father except through Me" (John 14:6).

The one who comes to Me I will by no means cast out (John 6:37).

Jesus Christ died on the cross and rose from the dead to pay the penalty for our sin and restore our lost relationship with God.

STEP 4: CONFESS YOUR SINS TO GOD AND ACCEPT JESUS CHRIST AS YOUR SAVIOR.

Here I am! I stand at the door and knock. If anyone hears my voice and opens the door, I will come in and eat with him, and he with me (Revelation 3:20, *NIV*).

If you confess with your mouth the Lord Jesus and believe in your heart that God has raised Him from the dead, you will be saved. For with the heart one believes unto righteousness, and with the mouth confession is made unto salvation. For "whoever calls on the name of the Lord shall be saved" (Romans 10:9, 10, 13).

You can receive Jesus Christ into your heart right now. Wherever you are, whoever you are, whatever you have done in the past, He will gladly come to your spirit and give you peace. His free gift of salvation is your only hope to find the answer to your lifelong quest for meaning and true happiness. He awaits your decision.

Will you sincerely pray this sinner's prayer with me?

> *Dear Lord Jesus, I acknowledge that I am a sinner and need your forgiveness. I believe You died for my sins. I want to turn from my sins and give You my heart. I repent of my sins and invite you to come into my life. I now trust you as Savior, and make you Lord of my life.* In Jesus' name. Amen.

If you have prayed this prayer sincerely, and you believe God has heard, you are saved! We believe with our hearts, then we tell others what God has done for us.

It is important to me to hear about your commitment to Christ and to celebrate with you! I want you to share your story with me. Write me a letter or send an e-mail and tell me when you made this decision to follow Christ and share with me the circumstances of this outstanding event. I will be praying for you that God will keep you and protect you in His great love.

Perry Stone, Jr.
PO BOX 3595
CLEVELAND, TN 37320-3595
E-Mail: *PerryStone@voe.org*

"You shall not be afraid of the terror by night, nor of the arrow that flies by day" (Psalm 91:5).

Appendix 1

Is the Antichrist a Jew from the Tribe of Dan?

As a teenage minister in the late 1970s, I began studying Biblical prophecy. At that time there seemed to be a consensus among evangelical ministers that the Antichrist would be a Jewish leader, rising up in the nation of Israel. They felt they could trace his linage to the tribe of Dan. Much of this concept was based on traditions and assumptions, rather than on direct scripture references. One main reason for this idea was that several prophecies—one from Daniel and another from Jesus himself—seems to indicate this. Daniel says:

> *He shall regard neither the God of his fathers nor the desire of women, nor regard any god; for he shall exalt himself above them all* (Daniel 11:37).

The phrase *God of his fathers* is a Hebraic phrase which alludes to the God of Abraham, Isaac and Jacob; or Yahweh God, who is the true God and the God of the Hebrew fathers. The assumption is this man, the Antichrist, must be Jewish because he does not honor the God of his fathers.

Understand that in the Islamic religion the Muslims name for God is Allah. Most Muslims will tell you that Allah is simply Arabic for God. Former Muslims and the more liberal Muslim scholars admit, however, that this name for God is not simply an Arabic name for the same God of Abraham. The early name for Allah was *Aliat*, the name of a moon deity worshiped in pre-Islamic times. This name does not honor the God of His fathers, for Ishamel and Esau's God was the same God of Abraham!

The second part of this traditional theory was that he must rise up out of the nation of Israel. This theory can be challenged with one main prophecy from the Book of Daniel. The ancient prophet saw the future empires of Bible prophecy. He saw how the Grecian empire would be divided into four parts:

Therefore the male goat grew very great; but when he became strong, the large horn was broken, and in place of it four notable ones came up toward the four winds of heaven (Daniel 8:8).

The male goat was a symbol of the great military leader, Alexander the Great, who seized the known world from the Persians and various other nations. After Alexander's death, his kingdom was divided to "the four winds," which alludes to the north, south, east and west. Alexander's kingdom was divided among his four generals:

- ◆ Cassander took the Grecian Empire
- ◆ Lysimachus took the Thracian Empire
- ◆ Seleucis took Mesopotamia and Iran
- ◆ Ptolomy I took the Egyptian Kingdom

And out of one of them came a little horn which grew exceedingly great toward the south, toward the east, and toward the Glorious Land (Daniel 8:9).

The imagery of the "little horn" is identified by scholars as being the future Antichrist. This prophecy plainly reveals that the Antichrist must come out of one of the areas where Alexander's kingdom was divided. The four choices are:

1. The area of Egypt and northern Africa
2. The area of Turkey
3. The area of Greece
4. The area of Syria

The Antichrist must come from one of these areas. The future world dictator will seize control of Egypt during his rule (Daniel 11:43). Turkey is the "king of the north" that will push against the Antichrist and his armies during the early part of the Tribulation (Daniel 11:40). This leaves only two regions: the area of Greece or the area of Syria. The Antichrist is identified in Biblical prophecy as the Assyrian or the Babylonian. Instead of coming from Israel, the Antichrist will invade Israel in the middle of the seven-year Tribulation. A Muslim, he will do this to liberate Palestine from the hands of the "infidels."

The third part of the theory says that the Antichrist must come from the tribe of Dan. This assumption is based primarily on the interpretation that the tribe of Dan is one of the tribes not mentioned in the listing of the 144,000 Jews in Revelation 7. This passage indicates that 12,000 Jews from 12 tribes will be sealed with the seal of God during the seven-year Tribulation.

The one main tribe not listed is the tribe of Dan. Based on a prophecy given in Genesis 49:17, and a commentary from one of the early church fathers stating the Antichrist will come from Dan, the Dan theory has been difficult to change in the minds of many prophecy students.

Having been to Israel 26 times, I can tell you something interesting about the area of the ancient tribe of Dan. The region is the area around modern Tel–Aviv. From a religious perspective, this area is filled with atheists and agnostics. Many Americans think that most Israelis are religious or Orthodox Jews. Only 18 percent of the population is orthodox.

One reason Dan may be missing is because the area of Dan, today, is filled with skeptics, atheists and agnostics.

During the early 1980s, many prophetic ministers began teaching that in the future, perhaps the Tribulation, the Jewish Temple would be rebuilt. They based this on three New Testament passages: Matthew 24:15; 2 Thessalonians 2:4; and Revelation 11:1, 2. The assumption was made that only a Jew could rebuild a Jewish Temple; if there is a Temple in the Tribulation, then, the Antichrist must be a Jew. This theory has problems for several reasons.

First, the final kingdom of prophecy is not a Jewish one but a Gentile one. The Bible indicates the Gentiles will tread the holy city (Jerusalem) underfoot for forty-two months (Revelation 11:2). *Second,* both previous Jewish temples were built with the assistance of Gentiles. Solomon used builders from Lebanon and the surrounding area in constructing his Temple. Herod the Great built a large addition to the Jewish Temple, and used non-Jewish workers in the process. The Jewish Temple can be built by using Gentiles, but must be dedicated by the Jews.

Who then, will be responsible for rebuilding the future Jewish Temple during the Tribulation? I believe the answer is the prophet Elijah. He will be one of the two witnesses sent to earth during the 42 months of the Tribulation (Revelation 11). Jesus announced that "Elijah is coming first and restores all things." Part of this restoration will be the initiation of a Jewish house of worship that will be completed in the middle of the Tribulation. This could be the trigger that will bring about the invasion of the Antichrist armies into Jerusalem!

Appendix 2

Is the Antichrist a Man of Peace or a Man of War?

I have heard various opinions and Biblical interpretations of the nature and character of the man identified in the writings of John and the early fathers as the Antichrist. This man will form a final end-time kingdom on earth and will be defeated when Christ returns to Jerusalem for the millennial reign (Revelation 20:1-4).

For many years ministers have expressed opinions that the Antichrist will be a man initiating peace across the world. They hold that he will be a problem-solver for humanity, and will be received as a Messiah by the entire world. In my early ministry I studied these views and began to parrot these ideas. As the years passed, however, I have come to believe that western Christianity has painted an unrealistic picture of this "man of sin." Where do we get the idea that he will be a man of peace? The **first reference** usually given to us is Daniel 9:27:

Then he shall confirm a covenant with many for one week; but in the middle of the week he shall bring an end to sacrifice and offering. And on the wing of abominations shall be one who makes desolate, even until the consummation, which is determined, is poured out on the desolate.

Evangelical scholars believe this verse refers to the Antichrist and his signing of a covenant or treaty during the final week, or seven years, of the Tribulation. What type of treaty is this? The assumption is that this is a peace treaty, although the word *peace* is not mentioned in the verse—or even in the entire chapter of Daniel 9. In reality, any treaty signed with Israel would be a land treaty, or a "land-for-peace" agreement. So we assume it is a peace covenant.

Daniel 8:25 says that this future leader "by peace shall destroy many." This word *peace* is not the common Hebrew word which is *shalom,* but the word *shalvah,* which alludes to having security. The Antichrist uses the promise of security to bring destruction to many people. This is what the apostle spoke about in 1 Thessalonians 5:3, when the apostle Paul spoke about the last days and the return of Christ:

For when they say, "Peace and safety!" then sudden destruction comes upon them, as labor pains upon a pregnant woman. And they shall not escape.

The initiation of a peace treaty and the concept of Middle East peace leads people to think the Antichrist will be a great man of peace. However, when reading about the first 42 months of the Tribulation, we read that there will be four horseman and riders, identified in Revelation 6, who introduce a time of great trial, war and famine to the earth. Notice that two of the four horsemen have swords:

Another horse, fiery red, went out. And it was granted to the one who sat on it to take peace from the earth, and that people should kill one another; and there was given to him a great sword.

I looked, and behold, a pale horse. And the name of him who sat on it was Death, and Hades followed with him. And power was given to them over a fourth of the earth, to kill with sword, with hunger, with death, and by the beasts of the earth (Revelation 6: 4, 8).

When the sword, which symbolizes war in the Bible, is released on earth, the power to kill one another indiscriminately is given to mankind. The sword in verse 8, mentioned with the pale horse and rider, indicates that instead of a world of peace during the first part of the Tribulation, there will be a series of wars and fighting!

The **second clue** as to the real nature of the coming Antichrist is revealed in Revelation 13. The man is identified by the symbolism of a beast rising up out of the sea (vv. 1, 2). In chapter 13, the beast (Antichrist) is a man of war. The Bible said he suffers a deadly wound to the head and is healed. The fact that this beast recovers from this deadly wound must be significant, since it is mentioned three times in this one chapter (Revelation 13:3, 12, 14). Many scholars believe the Antichrist was injured physically, or his empire was defeated and he comes back in a miraculous fashion to become a ruler in the final 42 months of the Tribulation. This is why John writes that the beast "was wounded by the sword [war] and lived" (v. 14).

Revelation 13 asks this question about the Antichrist, "Who can make war against the beast" (v. 4)? The fact is, the Book of Revelation indicates this man is a beast with the power of a sword [war] and is inspired and controlled by demonic power with a plan to kill and defeat his enemies (Revelation 13:2). In light of this, the concept that the final world dictator, the Antichrist, would be from a Muslim background is logical for the following reasons:

1. Islam rules much of the territory of ancient Biblical prophecy. Islam rules in Pakistan, Afghanistan, Iran, Iraq, Syria, Lebanon and Egypt. These are the prophetic lands of the ancient Biblical empires of Babylon, Media-Persia and Greece.

2. Islam has a major conflict with the Jews and Israel. Much of the Book of Revelation deals with activity in Israel and its people. Islam will attempt to annihilate the Jews in a final war.

3. Islam has a teaching called the "Sword of Islam." Islam will accept a false peace treaty with surrounding nations only until they have strengthened themselves to break the treaty and defeat their enemies. This "peace treaty" is a false treaty that will be broken in the middle of the seven years, by an Islamic leader who will unite a 10-nation coalition to control the oil of the Middle East and defeat Israel.

4. The idea that the world will enter some sort of utopia under the Antichrist is a western Christian theological tradition and is not the picture painted in either the Old or New Testament. Jesus spoke of the Tribulation, and said, "Unless those days were shortened, no flesh would be saved; but for the elect's sake those days will be shortened" (Matthew 24:22).

Instead of emphasizing that the Antichrist will be the head of economic prosperity by overseeing the European Union, it would be best to teach how his connection to Islam will bring about a false Islamic treaty that will eventually be broken and lead to major global conflicts. It will all climax in the visible return and reign of Christ!

Appendix 3

Attack on the Homeland: Future Terrorism in America

During the past 100 years, the world has passed through several different cycles of extreme difficulty. At the turn of the 20th century, the world saw the rise of Communism, a political ideology that eliminated the belief in God from their manifesto. Under Communism, millions of innocent people suffered and died at hands of dictators who theoretically made all people live on the same level but secretly padded their own pockets with wealth seized from others.

From the late 1920s into the mid-1940s, another "ism" resurfaced in the earth. This was Nazism, headed by Adolph Hitler, whose armies rolled over much of Europe, creating the Second World War. Hitler's dream was to build a blond-haired, blue-eyed, Arian race and an empire that would endure for 1,000 years. In the end, Nazi troops assisted in the murder and destruction of six million Jews and millions of Christians.

With the collapse of Communism in the Soviet Union and the defeat of Nazi Germany, many thought the world would enter a new era of peace and prosperity. It was felt that man would learn to live in peace beside his neighbor who was of a different race and religion. This image of the perfect global community was again shattered with the re-emergence of Islamic terrorism.

Few Americans were concerned about Middle East terrorism and its impact as long as the bombings and beheadings occurred halfway around the world. After 9/11, however, we began learning about terror training camps, sleeper cells and verses in the Qur'an that encouraged the beheading and killing of non-Muslims.

When it was discovered that the 19 hijackers on 9/11 had been living in America and were trained in our own flight schools, the term *sleeper cell* became a household word. Sleeper cells are individual groups, perhaps three to six in each group, who live as normal, common Americans, yet secretly plan attacks to be carried out on America soil.

Few Americans realize that not only were major arrests and interrogations made in the months since 9/11, but there have also been at least seven attacks stopped since 9/11. During one incident a policeman in New York noticed a strange design on a paper in an apartment. He recalled seeing the same design on a locker in the New York Subway. After investigating, authorities discovered that a high-powered plastic explosive was being stored in the area, with apparent plans to blow up a section of the subway.

In another incident a group of Middle Eastern men traveled from California to Florida by car to join a cruise. On arriving, they discovered their rooms were not on the same level on the boat, so they began arguing and demanded the lowest deck of the ship.

Alert police began questioning why they drove from California all the way to Florida for a cruise. Opening their luggage, they found large amounts of explosives with detonation devices. They planned to blow a hole in the ship when it was at sea!

While ministering in Maryland, I was invited by the host pastor to lunch in a restaurant in Delaware. As we passed a restaurant he began telling me a story related to him by a police officer who worked in the area. Before 9/11, the restaurant was owned by a group of Middle Eastern men. Shortly after 9/11, the restaurant was suddenly closed down and eventually sold. The new owners decided to tear out and replace the old walls. To their amazement they found weapons and cash hidden in bags behind the sheetrock. The restaurant was being used as a cover for some Islamic group who may have been preparing for some type of follow–up attack on American soil.

I have been told by a former worker in the federal government that there may be as many as 3,000 Muslims in America who are linked directly to terrorists. One of the great concerns is that these individuals may have entered the country before 9/11 on student visas; and since the visas expired, they have not been found. Because of the countries they are from and their names, government intelligence organizations are concerned they may be a part of dangerous sleeper cells.

Years ago a man told me of a group of Muslims from Morocco who were paid by their government to attend schools in America. When they arrived in America they were to call a number, leaving information of their location. In the event a major Jihad was called, they were to participate in it (this information was given to the proper authorities several years ago).

Having been to the Middle East, I realize that there are many Muslims who simply want a good job and hope to provide for their children. However, we must not underestimate the fact that it only takes a few fanatics to bring a dirty bomb or radiological weapon across the Mexican border and eventually detonate it in New York City or in the nation's capitol near our major federal buildings. Any dirty bomb could pollute the land for some time, rendering businesses helpless and impacting the economy for years to come.

Despite the lull between the storms and the defeat of so many in al Qaeda, Americans must remain vigilant. Perhaps this is another reason Jesus told us to "watch and pray!" We must keep our eyes open and pray without ceasing!

May God bless and keep you!

NOTES

NOTES